estre Executé. Suiuant

ix aoust qbq cinq. six

De Vau

le xx aoust 1656.

VAUX
LE
VICOMTE

VAUX LE VICOMTE

Jean-Marie Pérouse de Montclos

Photographs by Georges Fessy

Foreword by Marc Fumaroli

of the Académie française

Scala Books

Acknowledgements

Jean-Marie Pérouse de Montclos and Éditions Scala would like to thank the comte
and comtesse Patrice de Vogüé who enabled them to bring this project to a successful
conclusion by giving them free access to the archives of the château of Vaux-le-Vicomte.

Georges Fessy and Éditions Scala would like to express their heartfelt gratitude to Liliane
Desvergnes and all the staff at the château of Vaux-le-Vicomte for their kindness
and efficient help.

Éditions Scala would like to thank the following people for their assistance:
Christine André of the Prints Department at the Louvre and Catherine Bossis, Annie Madec
and Pierric Jean from the photographic service of the Réunion des Musées Nationaux.

First published in 1997 by Scala Books
an imprint of
Philip Wilson Publishers Ltd
143-149 Great Portland Street
London W1N 5FB

Distributed in the USA and Canada by
Antique Collectors' Club
Market Street
Industrial Park
Wappingers' Falls
New-York, NY 12590
USA

ISBN 1-857-59-173-9

© 1997 Éditions Scala, Paris

Translated from French by Judith Hayward
Design: Maxence Scherf
Layout and production: Frédéric Célestin
Picture research: Catherine Berthoud
Edited by Jane Bennett

Cover: *View of the château of Vaux-le-Vicomte from the statue of Hercules*

Endpapers: *Signature of Nicolas Foucquet, Louis Le Vau and the contractor Villedo,
on the back of the courtyard elevation on Le Vau's scheme in 1656*
Private collection

LIST OF CONTENTS

VAUX-LE-VICOMTE: A 'COURTESY' SPURNED BY LOUIS XIV

Vaux-le-Vicomte is a château that will for ever be associated with the memory of an entertainment. That entertainment on a night in high summer on 17 August 1661 was given at Vaux by Nicolas Foucquet, Superintendent of Finance to Louis XIV, for his king, the queen mother Anne of Austria and the French court.

Once the party was over and the lanterns had been extinguished, with its lord and master soon enmeshed in a snare, Vaux long remained silent and solitary like Sleeping Beauty. It could be said that this château, built with such care and speed, had fulfilled its purpose in the space of a few hours. That firework display, held against a latent backdrop of political drama, concluded the slow process started in the fifteenth century which transformed the great French feudal fortress, closed like a carapace, into an abode for leisure, open to the outside world.

Feudal fortresses were built to withstand a siege. The walls, moats, loopholes, battlements, towers and rampart walks were only the bare bones of a machine augmented by wooden and metal devices directed against enemy attacks. The lords that could shut themselves away in such fortresses were always ready to cross swords with rivals, invaders or even the king.

The process leading from the fortress to the château is the whole history of the French feudal aristocracy traced out in stone on the landscape. The transfiguration of a military caste into a leisured class, the shift from an ideal based on chivalry to one based on refined manners, produced a radical shift in the meaning and appearance of the French castle within two centuries. From being key elements of an economy based on feudal war, they moved to a central role in a monarchic economy based on leisure, and peace within the borders of the kingdom.

In the reign of Louis XIV the king became the only warlord, uniquely allowed to build fortresses. In Sébastien Le Prestre de Vauban he found a military engineer of genius who designed fortresses fit for a king, not on the scale of the local lord of the manor, but for an overall strategy dreamt up in Paris, then at Versailles, deploying the king's many, permanent, well equipped armies on the frontiers of the kingdom.

The metamorphosis of the fortress into a place of recreation was set in motion even before the Renaissance. It was apparent in the Gothic dreams woven from white stone which the miniatures in the *Très riches heures de Jean de Berry* show towering behind

peaceful scenes of rural life, following a rhythm imposed by seasonal tasks. It became spe-
cific in the châteaux built in the sixteenth century, translating the villas of Italian princes
and cardinals into the language of French masons and carpenters. The jewel of that
period is La Bastie d'Urfé, while its monument is Francis I's Fontainebleau. That development was given singular impetus between 1624 and 1642 by Cardinal Richelieu during his period as chief minister. The cardinal's onslaught against a feudal class that was
still alive and kicking, its thoughts turned back to war by contemporary religious conflict
and rebellion during Marie de Médicis's regency, led him to clear the French countryside
of castles. (More fortresses were destroyed due to him than châteaux were burnt down in
the French Revolution one and a half centuries later.) Thus the cardinal created a *tabula
rasa* conducive to the burgeoning of the 'modern' French château. Through this act of
vandalism Richelieu made it clear to the French nobility that the art of warfare was a
privilege exclusively reserved to royalty. The nobles were only entitled to practise this art
in the king's armies and there was no longer any use for their castles other than as places
to rest between campaigns carried out under the king's orders.

The château as a place of recreation matured in the reign of Louis XIII. Stripped of military trappings, keeping only a vestigial moat, it became established, was perfected and
spread as the cardinal made the authority of the state over the kingdom and its old aristocracy 'absolute' and universal. It symbolized the end of feudal freedom.

With the exception of the château of Blois, however, which Gaston d'Orléans left unfinished, this new generation of châteaux was not the handiwork of old families belonging
to the traditional soldierly nobility – who often adopted guerrilla tactics to resist the cardinal, or suffered under his harsh discipline. At best, when Richelieu did not take an axe
or a bludgeon to them, these families had to tolerate old-fashioned buildings on their
estates, legacies of the Middle Ages or the Renaissance. The initiative for these new
châteaux designed for leisure in the reign of Louis XIII came from the king's ministers
– the foremost lawyers, administrators and financiers. They used such buildings to display their often recently acquired wealth, their loyalty to the Crown to whom they owed
their prosperity and their attachment to a submissive concept of rest. Often these opu-
lent new country residences gave their owners a noble title which they acquired with the
estate on which they built. But even the 'innocent pleasures' which the duchesse de
Longueville, a supporter of the Fronde, said she disliked, were not always as innocent as
they seemed. From the reign of Louis XIII the old aristocracy, when not involved in
guerrilla tactics, invented its own leisure activities. Their 'country-house life' did not
merely entail a respectful separation between a public and a private sphere, as it did for
the cardinal's 'creatures', but it also displayed indifference towards those in government
and asserted the last preserve of aristocratic freedom: a private life possessed of its own

resources and capable of inventing entertainment without consulting the cardinal or the court. People like Henri de Montmorency or Gaston d'Orléans were both the last Renaissance princes and the first great eighteenth-century lords. Poets and writers who were experts in literary leisure helped them transform their free time into a busy, witty art form.

The model for this lifestyle, cut off from the court (in a town house where town life was practised, and in a château for leisure where it was possible to transpose that town life to the country), was provided in Paris from the start of Richelieu's period of office in 1624 by the marquise de Rambouillet. It was during that year that the poet Voiture, the secretary of the rebellious Gaston d'Orléans, became the prime mover in Mme de Rambouillet's famous 'Chambre bleue'. The marquise never went to court, liking neither Richelieu nor Louis XIII. Tallemant writes:

> "*From the age of twenty she no longer wanted to attend assemblies at the Louvre. She said she found nothing agreeable about just seeing how people pushed to get in and that sometimes she had chosen to go into a room to derive amusement from the bad order with which that kind of thing is done in France. It was not that she did not like entertainment, but she liked being entertained in private.*"

So Mme de Rambouillet created her own court. The spirit that reigned in her Salon was very different from that governing recreation in the houses and châteaux of Richelieu's 'creatures'. Descended from the Savellis, the wife of a Vivonne and the sister-in-law of the Cardinal of Rambouillet, she invented an economy of 'courteous' recreation for the old aristocracy, preserving its independence among chosen, trustworthy friends, all of which was alien to the 'bad order' prevailing at the Louvre. One day in the presence of Robert Arnauld d'Andilly she expressed this admirable wish:

> "*Very far from not doing everything in the world for my friends, if I knew there was a good and honest man in India, without knowing anything more about him, I would try to do everything I could to benefit him.*"

This art of living as a great lady was supported by the genius of the poet Vincent Voiture (1598-1648). Both knew how to attract into the same society high-born nobles impatient with life at court and literary figures not keen to serve the cardinal too closely. As Tallemant put it:

> "*It was the meeting-place for everything that was most courteous at court, and the most sophisticated minds of the century.*"

They all liked to meet and converse at either the marquise's town house in the rue Saint-Thomas-du-Louvre in Paris or the château of Rambouillet in the country, depending on the season. Rambouillet was an 'old-fashioned building' that she would have liked to replace with a 'fine house' if she had been 'in a position to spend large sums of money', like the minister and his 'creatures'. The gardens of R<ambouillet were the setting for agreeable entertainments, like the one described by Tallemant, dreamt up by the marquise to entertain her friend Philippe Cospéan, Bishop of Lisieux.

> *"At the château there is a very large meadow in the middle of which, by a quirk of nature, there is a virtual circle of large rocks between which stand tall trees providing very pleasant shade. It was here that Rabelais amused himself, according to local tradition; for the Cardinal du Bellay in whose service he was and M. de Rambouillet as close relations very often came and spent time at this house, and even today a certain hollow, smoke-darkened rock is called Rabelais's cooking-pot. So the Marquise suggested to M. de Lisieux that they should go for a stroll in the meadow. When he was close enough to the rocks to see through the leaves of the trees, he noticed something glimmering here and there. As he drew closer, it seemed to him that he could make out female forms, and that they were dressed as nymphs. To start with the Marquise pretended to see nothing of what he could see. Finally, having reached the rocks, they found Mlle de Rambouillet and all the young ladies of the house dressed as nymphs; seated on the rocks they were the most delightful sight in the world. The bishop was so captivated that ever afterwards he never saw the Marquise without mentioning the rocks of Rambouillet."*

Nothing illustrates this 'courtesy' better than the poetic inventions through which La Fontaine in *Le Songe de Vaux* brought to life the rooms of Foucquet's château and the various sites in the grounds that were still under construction. Foucquet, his wife Marie-Madeleine de Castille and their literary entourage – Pellisson, Madeleine de Scudéry, Mme de Sévigné, Jean de La Fontaine – styled themselves as the heirs to the *otium* of Mme de Rambouillet and Voiture, but on a different scale. In many respects Vaux-le-Vicomte was the realisation of Mme de Rambouillet's dream of the 'fine house'.

But Foucquet's château was also the most recent in that generation of châteaux for leisure which had been built in the wake of Cardinal Richelieu, his 'creatures' and his court. They grew in number after the cardinal's death, as did the fine new town houses in Paris under the 'good regency' of Anne of Austria. They increased again when the Fronde was over. Richelieu's château and famous gardens at Rueil, the château of président de Longueil at Maisons, the Plessis-Guénégaud château at Fresnes (the last two designed by François Mansart), the Plessis-Bellière château at Charenton and perhaps above all the château at Meudon for Abel Servien, (Foucquet's colleague and rival as joint Superintendent of Finance) formed a poetic rosary of which the admiring Mlle de Scudéry in her novel *Clélie* (1656-1661) counted the beads. Vaux was intended to outshine them all. But that splendour was to give a new, public authority to the spirit of courtesy and entertainment, which in the hands of Mme de Rambouillet had been the French aristocracy's most subtle retaliation against the tyrannical weight of Richelieu's 'absolute' government. It was like a posthumous revenge granted to the marquise.

In the new economy based on refined literary pastimes invented and disseminated by Mme de Rambouillet and Voiture, the château as a place of pleasure played a key role. In Mme Rambouillet's day it was just beginning. While they were unable to influence its architecture, the marquise and her poet invented its spirit, which was independent of the court. The progress of that spirit of gracious living was interrupted and stifled during the 'Grand siècle' by the king himself. He monopolized areas that even in the reign of Louis XIII and Anne of Austria had been part of private life and initiative. The leisure economy – Richelieu himself had not dreamt of trying to wrest control over this away from the marquise de Rambouillet – then became a matter for the king. Louis XIV was not content to be the 'king of war', summing up the military vocation of his nobles in his own person, he also wanted to be the king of noble leisure, its mainspring, centre and jealous master. The French economy based on this leisure was chilled for a long time by the king's attitude.

When the king travelled, the state, the administration, the army general staff and the members of the court always went with him. He was not a man, he was a leviathan. When the king who hated the city decided to 'relocate' his residence to the country at Versailles, he gradually created a huge administrative complex that also served as a general headquarters in the guise of a château. He multiplied second homes in the vicinity of Versailles but to no avail – the porcelain Trianon, the Grand Trianon, Marly – none of them worked. The Great King took all the machinations of his large court with him wherever he went. It was the very thing that the *divine Arthénice* when she dreamt of the château of leisure in her gardens at Rambouillet, or when it was described by La Fontaine in *Le Songe de Vaux*, set out to avoid at all costs. She had invisaged living in a small social circle of friends who knew how to enjoy themselves gracefully, naturally and wittily.

For a single night on 17 August 1661, to surprise and delight Louis XIV, Foucquet at Vaux brought off the *tour de force*. He combined the charm of a *fête galante*, such as Mme de Rambouillet might have devised for her guests, with the magnificence of a royal entertainment. That was the deeper meaning of the entertainment at Vaux, and of the château for which it had been built. That was its crime. Foucquet had wanted to reconcile two styles of leisure that were perhaps incompatible: the grace made possible by a private life of leisure, and the pomp demanded by the exercise of royal supremacy. The Superintendent had set out to bridge the rift that had opened up in Louis XIII's reign between the light-hearted society of friends that Mme de Rambouillet had gathered around her, and the anxiety-ridden, strictly supervised court with which Cardinal Richelieu surrounded the king. 'It is a fine thing to attempt unheard-of feats,' said Corneille's heroine Viriate in his play *Sertorius*. Vaux and its entertainment attempted to introduce the friendship and detachment of the life of leisure to the very centre of power. It was the idea of a poet states-man, and it faded as quickly as a rose.

The monumental entertainments devised by the duc de Saint-Aignan at Versailles in 1664 and 1668, using the same artists, would recover the royal magnificence of the entertain-ment staged at Vaux. But the grace and charm, intimidated by the grandeur of the king, had vanished. Foucquet and his friends had attempted the poetic folly of trying to com-bine the two. La Fontaine was wiser in the poem he devoted to Vaux, conjuring up private, delightful entertainments there, safe from the Gorgon stare of the state. For example he dreamt up a contest between the famous singer Michel Lambert and a dying swan in the canal of the château, to give pleasure to the mistress of the place, Marie-Madeleine de Castille, Mme Foucquet. La Fontaine gave her the Parnassan name Sylvia, just as Malherbe had conferred the name Arthénice on Mme de Rambouillet:

> *"Learning that a swan at Vaux was on the point of death Sylvia had sent in great haste for Lambert so as to compare his song with that of the poor swan... She sat down in an armchair beside the canal where the swan was and Lambert having first tuned his theorbo immediately sang a tune in his manner which was extremely beautiful... It was thought that the swan would not dare sing after him. However it did sing, and really sang quite well, but apart from the fact that the song was in a language which could not be understood, it was judged infe-rior by far to Lambert..."*

Neither in the entertainment given there by Foucquet for his king, nor in its architecture or decoration did Vaux want to make a choice between the intimate charm preferred by the master of the house and his friends, and a certain grandeur associated with the pres-ence of the king. Foucquet's utopia, an inheritance from the Italian courts and the court of the Valois kings, involved effecting a successful synthesis between the leisure economy and mainstream politics, between an aristocracy devoted to a life of leisure and a power-ful monarchy, itself tamed by refined ways and a smiling manner. The king preferred antithesis to synthesis. After Foucquet's fall from grace, Versailles put its full weight behind forgetting the gracious style of private leisure with which Vaux had vainly tried to invest royal majesty.

The Great Monarch had to reign for another half century before French aristocracy and its poets recovered sufficient independence to learn the lesson of Vaux. Even before 1715 there was no longer any question of reconciling private leisure with the majestic etiquette required for the king in the châteaux in the area around Paris. The aristocracy, emboldened by the advanced years of the lion of Versailles, was daring to think what Mme de Ram-bouillet had already fully understood and Foucquet had tried to deny one last time: that the happiness of private life was incompatible with the grandeur of the state. When the Commander is invited along, a private party turns into a petrified feast.

The eighteenth century got under way at Sceaux from 1711 with the night-time entertainments given by the duchesse du Maine, and it immediately ran counter to Versailles and Marly. With added liveliness and freedom it reinvented Rambouillet and the 'Chambre bleue', Vaux and the *chambre des Muses*. It created a *rocaille* civilization, and even today countless châteaux, near Paris, Rouen, Dijon, Bordeaux and Toulouse, bear witness to the gracious lifestyle for which they were built, decorated and furnished. In search of the capitals of this civilization based on leisure we must turn to Lunéville built for Stanislas Leczinsky, the idle king of Lorraine, and Chanteloup belonging to Louis XV's disgraced minister, the duc de Choiseul. Louis XV moved back to Versailles on the death of the Regent, the duc d'Orléans; there, in the forbidding setting devised by and for his great-grandfather, he was reduced to copying part time and in secret the gracious lifestyle which his subjects had learnt to practise without the slightest concern about involving their king, as Foucquet had felt he must do.

Less than a month separated the dreadful day of 5 September when Louis XIV had Superintendent Foucquet arrested in the city of Nantes, (secretly put in a state of siege) and that night of 17 August 1661 immortalized in the description of it a few days later by Jean de La Fontaine for his friend Maucroix:

> *We started with a walk. The whole court took great pleasure in watching the display of water. Vaux will never be more beautiful than it was that evening. [...] The waterfall, the* Gerbe d'eau, *the* Fontaine de la Couronne *and the Animals all vied with one another over which would be most admired; the ladies for their part did no less.*
>
> > *One and all with regard to beauty*
> > *Contested each in her own manner;*
> > *The Queen vied with her sons over who would be kindest,*
> > *And Madame tried to outshine the light."*
>
> *I observed one thing which was not perhaps sufficiently noted: it is that the Nymphs of Vaux always had their eyes on the king; his health and good looks ravished them all, if we may employ such a word in talking of such a great prince.*
>
> *Following the walk we went and had supper. The delicacy and choiceness of the dishes served were outstanding; but the graciousness with which the Superintendent and his wife did the honours of their house was even more so.*
>
> *Once supper was over it was the turn of the play: a stage had been erected at the bottom of the* allée des sapins.
>
> > *In this place which is not the least lovely*
> > *Of those contained in such a delectable spot,*
> > *At the foot of these pines and beneath the* grille d'eau,
> > *Amidst the pleasant coolness*

Of the woodland fountains, shade and breezes,

The pleasures were prepared

That we savoured that night.

The stage was adorned with thick foliage,

And illuminated by a hundred torches:

The Heavens were jealous. Finally just imagine

That when the curtains were drawn,

Everything at Vaux conspired to please the king:

The music, water display, the lights, the stars.

The decorations were magnificent and it could not all be done without using mechanical devices.

We saw rocks open and terms move,

And many a figure turn on its pedestal.

Two enchanters full of skill

Did so much through their imposture

That we believed they had the power

To command nature:

One of these enchanters is Monsieur Torelli,

An expert magician and performer of miracles;

And the other is Le Brun: Vaux embellished by him

Affords a thousand rare spectacles to onlookers:

Le Brun whose mind and hand we admire,

Father of attractive and beautiful inventions,

Rival of Raphael and his like, successor of Apelles,

Through whom our climate owes nothing to that of Rome;

Through the wit of these two the thing was arranged.

First before the eyes of those assembled

Such a well made rock appeared

That we thought it really was a rock;

But as it imperceptibly changed into a shell,

A lovely Nymph emerged from it

Looking like the actress Béjart,

A Nymph excelling in her art,

Not surpassed by any other.

Thus she recited with great grace

A prologue thought to be one of the finest

That could be written in this genre,

And finer than I say,

Or in fact than I dare say:

For it is in the style

Of our friend Pellisson.

Thus though I admire it,

I will stay silent since it is not permissible

To praise one's friends.

(Translation of Jean de La Fontaine, *Lettre à M. de Maucroix*, account of an entertainment given at Vaux, 22 August 1661, *Œuvres diverses*, Pierre Clarac, Paris, Gallimard, La Pléiade, 1958, pp. 523-525)

Superintendent Foucquet, a well educated magistrate, a brilliant and respected financier and an enlightened patron of the arts, secretly imprisoned, and charged with capital offences (peculation, lese-majesty), seemed at first to have no means of saving himself. The public was up in arms against the minister whom Louis XIV would describe in his *Mémoires* as a 'thief'. With heartrending lyricism in the *Élégie aux Nymphes de Vaux*, which brave friends of the imprisoned Superintendent circulated in anonymous pamphlets during 1662, La Fontaine associates – a poet's idea – the memory of beauty and pity in the face of misfortune; in their name he pleads for royal mercy:

Fill the air with cries in your deep grottoes;

Weep, Nymphs of Vaux, enlarge your waves,

And may the swollen Anqueil ravage the treasures

With which the gaze of Flora has beautified its banks.

Your innocent tears will not be condemned;

You can give way to your oppressive grief:

Everyone expects this generous duty of you;

The Fates are happy: Oronte is wretched.

You saw him only recently beside your fountains,

Unafraid of the uncertain favours of Destiny,

Full of brilliance, full of fame, adored by mortals,

Receiving honours due only to altars.

Alas! how he has fallen from this supreme happiness!

How different you would find him from himself!

For him the finest days are second nights:

Devouring cares, regrets, troubles,

Ill-fated guests of his sad abode,

Plunge him constantly into abysses of affliction.

(Translation of Jean de La Fontaine, *Élégie pour M.(onsieur) F.(oucquet)*, *Œuvres diverses*, Paris, Gallimard, La Pléiade, 1958, p. 528)

Born into a family of merchants and well educated magistrates, through his birth, his education at the hands of the Jesuits, his profession and personal temperament, Nicolas Foucquet was a jurist, financier and diplomat: the very opposite of a soldier. On the other hand he was perfectly capable of assimilating the new aristocratic ideal of the well-bred gentleman. Like most of the major figures associated with the Parlement, known as the *Grande Robe* (high-ranking officials), whose offices could be bought, he combined legal and literary culture with a keen business sense, which he deployed in administering the king's finances. He used the huge personal credit he had built up in the Paris market to benefit the court, which was hard pressed financially during the worst years of the Fronde. He was then able to buy the office of *Procureur général du Parlement* (Attorney General) in 1650, and in 1654 it led to his appointment as Superintendent of Finance. This role he first shared with his rival Abel Servien, like himself from the *Grande Robe*, a member of the Académie française and the signatory of the Treaty of Munster – learning from the Fronde. Foucquet's loyalty to the young king could no more be doubted than the extent of the credit he enjoyed. More than anyone else he had financed the victory of the king and Mazarin, both on France's external frontiers against the Imperial forces and the Spanish and internally against the Fronde. In his position as *Procureur général* in 1649-1652 he had played a decisive political role in splitting the refractory magistrates, isolating the princes supporting the Fronde, restoring royal authority and breaking up the factions.

His talents seemed to designate him for the job of chief minister to the young king when the time came. A growing rumour which he did not deny assumed that he would be Mazarin's successor, especially after the death of Abel Servien in 1659.

Since the assassination of 'good king Henri' (Henry IV) there had been no moral or political respite in France. After Richelieu had taken the country into the Thirty Years' War in 1635, the French under the constraint of a virtual dictatorship had had to sustain a war effort and accept the fiscal sacrifices which led the Parlement to rebel in 1658 and the princes to follow suit in 1651. The end of the Fronde, the Peace of the Pyrenees in 1660 and Louis XIV's marriage to the Spanish Infanta Marie-Thérèse, ensured that France would have a leading role in Europe. It prompted the French to dream of a reign that would at last be peaceful and fruitful, in which the 'fundamental laws of the kingdom' overridden by Richelieu's 'modern policy' would be restored.

The clever and charming Superintendent of Finance who had done so much to re-establish the king's full authority in France, seemed to combine in his person all that was promised by this expectation of a golden age. He gathered ever more supporters around him. Since his almost miraculous birth great hopes had been vested in the young king himself, and it seemed impossible for him to find a chief minister more in tune with what France expected of him.

Foucquet wanted to articulate the peaceful, prosperous days lying ahead in a language the French knew well, the language of the château. As soon as he was appointed Superintendent in 1653 he set about building a château at Vaux-le-Vicomte on the site of an old feudal fortress, on a noble estate which he had bought in 1642 and enlarged ever since.

Vaux sums up the economy and philosophy of gentlemanly leisure which had taken shape between 1630 and 1642 as a counterbalance to the war economy and the philosophy of obedience imposed by Cardinal Richelieu. It is one of those 'Louis XIII châteaux' devised as a preserve for private 'recreation' in a kingdom mobilized by the fearsome cardinal. But with a new political programme and the promise of demobilization within the kingdom, Vaux was intended to be something more: a setting for a Royal Entrance through which Louis XIV would pass to lead France, advised by Foucquet, into an era of plenty and gracious comfort.

The plans for Vaux did not really take on their final form until 1656. Work progressed under the supervision of the architect Louis Le Vau, while at the same time the Superintendent's chances of succeeding Mazarin seemed to increase. To devote himself entirely to Foucquet's commission, Le Vau abandoned the building work in progress at the Hôtel Lambert de Thorigny in Paris. In 1659 the same Le Vau left the renovations at the château of Meudon – formerly the property of the Guise family – unfinished on the death of Abel Servien, the second Superintendent of Finance. (Building work there had started in 1655, rivalling Vaux and just as ambitious in scale.)

From 1656 when Superintendent Foucquet took on Paul Pellisson, a very talented young lawyer, as his 'chief clerk'. With unerring taste Pellisson selected the most gifted artists of the '1660 generation' for his employer, setting them to work with the architect Le Vau. Together they would turn the château, its gardens and its interior decoration into a synthesis and symbol of Foucquet's programme for the country: moderation in power, charm in authority. Charles Le Brun, to whom Foucquet entrusted direction of the tapestry works at Maincy near Vaux in 1658, was at the same time commissioned to undertake the painted decoration of the château then being built.

Since the death of the two leading painters in Paris – Laurent de La Hyre and Simon Vouet – Le Brun who had spent time in Rome studying the example of Nicolas Poussin had come to the fore as the leader of the school. Like the Italian artists Pietro da Cortona and Romanelli, he was able to design large decorative interiors scheme which were better than Poussin's, and like the Italians he knew how to direct a team of artists.

At Vaux, while waiting for the chance to excel in the grand genre of 'Historical Painting' for Louis XIV's palaces under Colbert, Le Brun retained the proper measure of grace and elegance which had been prevalent in the fine private houses built in and around Paris in the reign of Louis XIII and during the regency of Anne of Austria.

Apollo should have been featured on the dome of the large central salon of the château. The Muses, addressed in poetry by La Fontaine, were depicted by Le Brun on the ceiling of the room that bears their name. This room, hung with tapestries, should have become the equivalent of the marquise de Rambouillet's 'Chambre bleue' in Paris – which owed its name to a series of floral tapestries lining its walls – in a style appropriate to the kingdom governed by Foucquet. In *Le Songe de Vaux* La Fontaine was worried about this already perilous change of scale: in his eyes it ran the risk of sterilizing the freedom and naturalness that favoured the nurture of literature and the arts:

> *"What? I find you here, my divine mistresses?*
>
> *You are no longer residing in your remote mountains?*
>
> *What charm has the panelling I see held for you?*
>
> *It was said that you loved the silence of the woods,*
>
> *Who has led you to depart from that solitary mood?*
>
> *How have palaces come to appeal to you?*
>
> *In vain I had sought you on the banks of a stream,*
>
> *But what celebration causes such new luxury?*
>
> *Why are you dressed in such a striking garb?*
>
> *Muses, what have you done with your loose robes,*
>
> *In which in the woods, without ever tiring,*
>
> *Amidst the court of the animals you could be seen dancing:*
>
> *I find something disconcerting about such a great change."*

The sculptors Michel Anguier, François Girardon, Pierre Puget, Thibaut Poissant and Jacques Sarrazin were employed to provide the allegorical decoration of the château and the paths in its park. The gardeners Le Nôtre and La Quintinie presided over the design of the landscaped park and the kitchen gardens. Vaux was intended to offer a synthesis of French taste, as it had matured in private houses under the influence of Italy since the 1630s. It was intended to symbolize the peaceful, prosperous future, a future of leisure dedicated to literature and the arts, which Foucquet had in mind for the king and his kingdom. The poet Jean de La Fontaine, a friend of Pellisson's for twenty years, was given the task of writing the poem that would sum up the château's significance. André Félibien, a historian and art critic, a friend of Poussin whom Foucquet had asked to design antique-style terms for the park of his château, started writing a description in prose of this French Parnassus.

Therefore we should not see Vaux, still unfinished in 1661, as a 'transition' foreshadowing the 'perfection' of Versailles. First of all Versailles never was 'perfect'. In the reign of Louis XIV there were several versions of Versailles which show a building site. The Versailles of Le Vau and Le Nôtre after 1661, enlarging the hunting lodge that Louis XIII had loved, was inevitably a magnified version of the minister's château, given that the same architect, gardener and landscape gardener were involved. Louis XIV's first response to Vaux was to copy it on a royal scale. The 'grand taste' of the 'Grand siècle' did not become established at Versailles, giving the royal palace its original appearance, until the genius of Jules-Hardouin Mansart succeeded in expressing the majesty of Louis XIV in his maturity.

Thus the Vaux of Le Vau and the Versailles of Mansart, a generation later, cannot be compared. They are two masterpieces of an entirely different order. One – Vaux – is a private château: Foucquet had undoubtedly devised it as a 'courtesy' (in the sense the word was given by the marquise de Rambouillet). He intended to offer it to the king as a proof of his friendship and gratitude when he was promoted to the rank of chief minister, and he had wanted it to be worthy of Louis XIV. But this gift intended for a king retains the proportions and charm of a large private house. The other – Mansart's Versailles – is a royal palace designed for 'the greatest king in the world', his court and his government.

If Louis XIV is already present at Vaux it is as a reflection, as he was seen by his Superintendent who hoped to become his chief minister: a 'great king', but one who knew how to share the pleasures of his subjects and looked for his greatness in the happiness and repose of private citizens. This imaginary Louis XIV, dreamt of by Foucquet and his friends, still reigns at Vaux today, in the château and the gardens, the hero of an entertainment that was all the more wonderful because it had no tomorrow.

Marc FUMAROLI
of the Académie française

The commission

Nicolas Foucquet's career • His role as a patron of literature and science
The artists at Vaux • The trial and sentencing of Nicolas Foucquet

The château of Vaux-le-Vicomte owes its name to the convergence of two valleys on a noble estate, its reputation to the collaboration of first-rate artists and the concerted efforts of famous writers, and its legend to the conjunction of great good fortune and ill-fortune, both affecting Nicolas Foucquet.

Foucquet had been Louis XIV's Superintendent of Finance, yet he died in prison; he was accused by the state, but exonerated by public opinion; when powerful he was so adulated that he even featured in a novel as one of the heroes, and after his death he periodically resurfaced as the mysterious prisoner in the iron mask; finally Foucquet has been seen by historical criticism as the first victim of nascent absolutism.

The Foucquets were a bourgeois family from Anjou who climbed the social ladder rapidly. Nicolas's father François sold his office as a *conseiller* [judge] at the Parlement [High Court of Justice] and bought the office of *maître des requêtes* [legal adviser] which meant that he served the person in power, in his particular case Cardinal Richelieu, whom he seconded in his maritime and colonial undertakings. He chose the family emblem, the squirrel (called a 'fouquet' in Anjou), and the motto 'quo non ascendet' (whither will he not climb) which Nicolas's enemies changed to 'quo non ascendam' (whither will I not climb?). His mother Marie de Maupeou also belonged to an influential family with links to the Parlement. The two had fif-

---

Coving in the chambre des Muses

The Foucquets' motto 'Quo non ascendet' (whither will he not climb?)
appears throughout the decoration, the motto of a family rapidly
ascending the social ladder, with the squirrel as its symbol.
Foucquet's enemies read it as 'Quo non ascendam'
(where will I not climb to?), a travestied form of the motto
which apparently very much irritated Louis XIV on his visits to Vaux.

Portrait of Nicolas Foucquet, vicomte de Vaux,
marquis de Belle-Isle (1615-1680), by Robert Nanteuil, 1661

The engraving dates from the downfall of Nicolas Foucquet, Superintendent of Finance. It was also the year of Mazarin's death and of Louis XIV's personal assumption of power. Nicolas Foucquet, accused of diverting public funds and plotting against the king, was to die in the prison of Pignerol in 1680. Legend has confused him with the mysterious prisoner known as the Man in the Iron Mask, because he was forced always to wear a mask, who arrived at Pignerol in 1679 and died several years later at the Bastille.

Foucquet was Superintendent of Finance, (i.e. more of a banker to the king than a Minister of Finance) from 1653 to 1661. He staked his considerable personal fortune to sustain the credit of the state which had been undermined by civil and foreign wars. He was loyal to the king during the Fronde whereas his links with the Parlement might have been expected to lead him to side with the rebels. At the height of his power he provided pensions for famous writers ranging from Corneille to La Fontaine, and employed artists to work on the château of Vaux-le-Vicomte, his supreme achievement.

The engraver Robert Nanteuil (1623-1678) produced portraits of all members of high society in the mid-seventeenth century. At the bottom of the engraving are Foucquet's coat of arms: the squirrel (a 'fouquet' in the Anjou dialect), the marquis's coronet and two supporting lions.

Messire Nicolas Foucquet = Chevalier, Vicomte de Melun
et de Vaux, Conseiller du = Roy en ses conseils, Ministre
d'Estat, Surintendant des = finances et Procureur General
de sa Majesté

R. Nanteuil ad vivum pinx. et sculpebat 166.

The Foucquets' monogram

The F and reversed F entwined
produce the C of Marie-Madeleine de Castille,
Nicolas Foucquet's second wife.
Sometimes the monogram is traversed by an arrow
which is probably the symbol of conjugal love.
It is set against olive branches, an evocation of the peace re-established
partly due to the Superintendent's efforts.

The squirrel in the Foucquets' coat of arms

The tablets above the windows on the façade overlooking the entrance
courtyard are decorated with various motifs.
Here the squirrel is depicted in a laurel wreath,
and the supporting lions in the coat of arms are treated realistically,
not according to heraldic conventions.

Lions at the bottom of the stairs framing the grotto

In their paws the lions hold a horn of plenty, symbol of the prosperity owed to the Superintendent,
and the squirrel, the Foucquets' emblem.
The lions are from Foucquet's coat of arms; but contemporaries identified them with the king himself
protecting his loyal minister. Fate was written in these figures:
in the end the lion brought down the squirrel that had sought to climb so high.

teen children twelve of whom survived: the girls entered convents, and the boys' hair was tonsured. Religion was part of their heritage. The Foucquets were committed to fighting on behalf of the Counter-Reformation; they were patrons of the new Order of the Visitation whose almoner in Paris was St Vincent de Paul; they were close to the Jesuits who were responsible for Nicolas's education.

Nicolas Foucquet was born in 1615, belonging to the same generation as the three artists who were to create the château of Vaux: the architect Louis Le Vau (1612-70), the gardener André Le Nôtre (1613-1700), and the painter Charles Le Brun (1619-90). He was educated at the Collège de Clermont, a famous Jesuit school in Paris. In 1635 he bought the office of maître des requêtes. In 1640 he married Louise Fourché, the daughter of a rich parliamentarian who brought a fine dowry with her. His father died that same year. A year later his wife died, leaving substantial financial means at his disposal. The purchase of the old château of Vaux-le-Vicomte on 1 February 1641 marked the start of a policy of buying up land which enabled him to establish a sizeable estate within twenty years. In 1650 he bought the office of *procureur général* (Attorney General) at the Parlement, making him the king's representative at the High Court. During the Fronde he remained loyal to the young king, the Queen Regent and her Prime Minister, Cardinal Mazarin.

The Fronde, an uprising that lasted for four years (1648-1652), tended to challenge Richelieu's achievements. The high nobility and office-holders wanted to exploit the king's minority and Mazarin's unpopularity to regain their full privileges. These nobles, 'les Grands', were the descendants of the great feudal overlords, while the office-holders were those who had purchased their positions (i.e. they owned part of the state's authority). The gradual installation of a new administration controlled by *intendants* [appointed administrators] was a threat to the privileges of both groups. Parliamentarians were very much to the fore among the office-holders. The refusal of the Parlement in Paris to register a royal decree spread the miseries of war throughout France. A terrifying image of the horrors that resulted from this instability was produced by the engraver Jacques Callot (1592/3-1635). Foucquet's fortune was built up during this time of turmoil. His loyalty to the king, however surprising it might seem on the part of an eminent office-holder, was not based merely on the intuition of a speculator with a good eye for long-term investment, but perhaps even more so upon an involvement in Richelieu's achievements in which the Foucquets had played a part.

On 4 February 1651 Nicolas Foucquet married Marie-Madeleine de Castille, the very richly endowed daughter of an extremely wealthy parliamentarian. In 1653

*Panel of the wainscotting
in the dining-room*

The interior decoration
has many compositions that play
on the heraldic emblems of Nicolas Foucquet
(the squirrel) and his wife Marie-Madeleine
de Castille (the tower).

he was appointed Superintendent, in conjunction with Abel Servien, which gave him control over the finances of the state. This appointment was a reward for his loyalty and acknowledged his competence, but the fact that he shared it with Servien indicates Mazarin's latent hostility - his huge personal expenditure depended far too much on Foucquet's credit. In 1654 Foucquet bought the house of Saint-Mandé near the château de Vincennes, the Cardinal's residence[1], and in 1658 the island of Belle-Isle off southern Brittany. This acquisition enabled him to develop the shipping and colonial business founded by his father and to become one of France's foremost ship-owners. When Servien died in February 1659 Foucquet was solely responsible for finance, and on Mazarin's death in 1661 he was motivated by an ambition to become Prime Minister. But 1661 was to be the year of his downfall, for which Colbert had been preparing a long time.

Colbert had moved from Mazarin's service into the service of the king, convincing him that his Superintendent of Finance was robbing him and plotting against him. Colbert wanted Foucquet's position, and he would get it. History has described this succession as integrity driving out knavery, painstaking service to the state replacing pliancy and prevarication. In fact Colbert's policy differed from Foucquet's less through its content than through its context, in which the king had properly re-established his authority.

One of the many proofs of this is the maritime and colonial policy pursued by Foucquet, between Richelieu and Colbert; the three of them founded the French colonial empire by encouraging the development of trading and seafaring companies. This explains the purchase of Belle-Isle. Foucquet, marquis de Belle-Isle, could have laid claim to a finer title than that of Prime Minister, and one far better suited to his strange fate: the title of Viceroy of the West Indies! In September 1660 he had secretly purchased the title of Viceroy and Lieutenant-General of all the islands, shores, harbours, coasts and mainland in southern and northern America; being canny he wanted to wait for a propitious moment, so had it transferred to the marquis de Feuquières - his nominee remained in possession of this borrowed distinction.[2]

The novelist Paul Morand, who became infatuated with Foucquet, made the following pen-portrait of him: 'Brilliant, devious, worldly, a master of compromise, casuistical, with an unbeatable memory for Latin lines, a lover of clever mottos, drawn like a moth to the flame at every entertainment, Foucquet is the archetypal product of the Parisian Jesuits (in the provinces, things were different: the Jesuits of Rheims were to produce Colbert). The spiralling rise... and ultimately the great broken arc is very much Jesuit architecture, and Foucquet's very life'.[3] The comparison which displays an obvious prejudice with respect to the morality and Jesuit piety which Foucquet perfectly exemplified, also betrays a certain ignorance of what Jesuit architecture in France in the first half of the seventeenth century was really like. In dealing with its buildings the Company of Jesus, like any business, was first and foremost concerned with economy and efficiency. For a long time the use of the adjective 'Jesuit' as a synonym for 'Baroque' obscured that fact. This did not mean that gold could not be put on altars as a way to encourage admiring surges of piety. Foucquet acted no differently, but for the benefit of his own undertakings.

Contemporary engraved or painted portraits no doubt present better likenesses than Morand's written portrait. The main engraved portraits are the work of Gilles Rousselet in 1659, Claude Mellan in 1661 and Robert Nanteuil[4], the same year. It has been said that Philippe de Champaigne and Pierre Mignard also produced portraits of Foucquet, but if so their work has been lost.[5] The fine portrait of a man at the château of Versailles is no longer thought to be by Sébastien Bourdon, or to depict Foucquet.[6] While the portrait by Charles Le Brun is known only through an engraving by François de Poilly. The only painted por-

Beauty clipping Cupid's wings by Charles Le Brun

Beauty, depicted with Madame Foucquet's features,
is clipping Cupid's wings so that he will 'always remain close to her as domestic love
which must not carry his weapons beyond the threshold of the house' (A. Félibien).
She is assisted by Minerva, or Wisdom, and by Hymen bearing a torch and a squirrel.
The picture which is an allegory of conjugal fidelity might have been painted
shortly after Nicolas Foucquet's marriage to Marie-Madeleine de Castille in 1651.

trait to have been preserved, now at Vaux, used to be attributed to Louis Fernand Elle[7] and there are obvious similarities between it and Poilly's engraving. The engraver Bertinetti, who was a protégé of Foucquet, left a medal depicting the Superintendent, oddly dated 1665, which would have been after his downfall.[8] These portraits cannot be regarded as masterpieces of French art, but they portray a masterpiece – the Superintendent himself. For as Marc Fumaroli notes, that was how major seventeenth-century personalities were depicted by the artists and poets of the next century.[9]

The features of Marie-Madeleine de Castille are believed to have been borrowed for two paintings by Le Brun. The first picture of Mary Magdalene was intended for the chapel of Vaux.[10] The second, depicting *Beauty clipping Cupid's wings*[11] is a fine introduction to art at the château, still deeply imbued with preciosity. Minerva, the goddess of wisdom, is shown assisting Beauty. While Hymen with the squirrel of the Foucquets on his shoulder illuminates the scene. The historiographer André Félibien, who sat at table with the Foucquets and was the exegetist of the decorative scheme at Vaux, supplied the key to this picture which he saw at the château: 'Domestic love must never carry its weapons beyond the walls of the house!'[12] The idea was no doubt taken from *Mercury clipping Cupid's wings before Venus*, a composition by Eustache Le Sueur (1617-55) for the *salon des Muses* at the Hôtel Lambert, a work Le Brun would have known well since he had taken part in decorating that house. Finally, according to Guillet de Saint-Georges, the historiographer from the Académie royale de peinture et de sculpture, [13] Michel Anguier sculpted a figure of Charity modelled on Madame Foucquet, but this was for the house at Saint-Mandé. All witnesses portray her as a dignified and beautiful woman, admittedly rather haughty, but that would enable her to hold her head high when put to the test.

The fact that a wife has an inspiring image is no guarantee of her husband's good behaviour. The comment made by the treacherous Abbé de Choisy is well known: 'Foucquet pretended to work alone in his office at Saint-Mandé and while the whole Court... was in his antechamber loudly singing the praises of the great man for his tireless work he used a secret staircase to slip down to a little garden where his nymphs... came to keep him company in return for gold.'[14] A great many rumours circulated regarding Foucquet's love life. It is almost certain that he paid court to the marquise de Sévigné and that she turned him down. He was purportedly audacious enough to tackle Louise de La Vallière, about to become the object of the king's affections: at the very least he sought to gain her support by flattering her. Whatever the truth, at the time of the trial letters from women were

Mademoiselle de Scudéry (1607-1701)

A literary figure, known as Sappho in the salons
frequented by the *précieux and précieuses*,
she wrote several long serial
novels including *Cléomine, histoire romaine*,
where Nicolas Foucquet appears
under the name of Cléomine,
and Le Brun as Méléandre;
Vaux-le-Vicomte is described in it as Valtère.

Paul Pellisson (1624-1693)

The smallpox which disfigured Pellisson,
diverting him from a career as an advocate
and turning him towards literature,
did not prevent him from becoming Madeleine
de Scudéry's sweetheart. Employed by Foucquet
as a head clerk, he had the special responsibility
of keeping the list of pensions paid to writers
under the Superintendent's protection.

found at Saint-Mandé and these were used by the prosecution to discredit Foucquet and turn society ladies, worried about their reputations, against him. 'I hate sin, but I fear need even more: so come and see me soon' – this anonymous declaration could be attributed to any lady at Court.

Foucquet's role as a patron of science and literature was no doubt his best long-term investment. For as Voltaire was to observe when witing about Foucquet's trial in his *Le Siècle de Louis XIV* of 1751, 'it was to be writers who saved his life'. Patronage was part of the way society worked under the *Ancien Régime*. Without it writers and scientists would not have survived. Pensions were given in exchange for flattering dedications. People under an obligation and close family friends met in their patrons' drawing-rooms, that of the marquise du Plessis-Bellière, Foucquet's best friend, or at the house at Saint-Mandé. The Superintendent's lists featured many names which now mean little or nothing to us: Cossart, Deschampsneufs, Rapin, Boisrobert, Brebeuf, Hesnault, Gombault, Cureau de La Chambre, Ménage. Do we

La Fontaine (1621-1695)

Molière (1622-1673)

Madame de Sévigné (1626-1696)

Tormented by money problems,
La Fontaine sought Foucquet's protection
by dedicating *Adonis*, a poem describing society
in love with the gods, to him.
When asked to describe the wonders of Vaux
in verse, he embarked on *Le Songe de Vaux*,
a commission he did not finish.

On 12 July 1661 Molière staged a performance
of *L'École des maris* in the alcove of the *chambre
des Muses* at Vaux before Queen Henrietta Maria
of England, Madame and Monsieur. At the end
of the month Foucquet commissioned another
play from him, which he wrote and produced in
a fortnight. It was *Les Fâcheux*, performed before
the king at the entertainment of 17 August 1661.

It is not known when Madame de Sévigné
and Foucquet first met. Their families came
from Brittany and both worshipped
at the church of the Visitation
and this may have brought them together
at a very early stage. It is clear however that
by 1657 Foucquet had resigned himself
to enjoying no more than her friendship.

remember that Scarron wrote *Le Roman comique*, or that Quinault was a writer of tragedies whose reputation equalled Corneille's? A few of these forgotten names deserve special mention because of the role they played in Foucquet's life: the doctor Jean Pecquet, whose theories about the circulation of the blood followed those of Harvey, became his steward; Jean Loret, the rhyming gazette-writer, recorded the feats of the public man in the *Muze historique;* the writer Paul Pellisson was called the 'notary of Parnassus' because as Foucquet's confidential agent he was in charge of the list of pensions; and in particular Madeleine de Scudéry, known as Sappho to the adherents of preciosity, who wrote *Artamène* ou *le Grand Cyrus* (1649-53) or *Clélie, histoire romaine* (1654-1661), long novels published in serial form. *Clélie* included the famous 'Carte du Tendre which taught the path that could be followed to travel from New Friendship to Tenderness', a journey Nicolas must have made on several occasions. He himself is featured in Volume XI (1660) of the book as Cléomine, while Vaux appears as Valtère and Le Brun as Méléandre. His famous protégés included Charles Perrault, Thomas Corneille and Pierre Corneille whom Foucquet encouraged to return to tragedy after a long silence. In his notice to the reader of *Œdipe* (1659), the tragedy commissioned by Foucquet, Pierre Corneille writes: 'Everyone knows that this great Minister is the Superintendent of Literature as much as of Finance; that his house is as open to thinkers and creative artists as it is to businessmen... but everybody does not know that his bounty has extended to reanimating Muses that have been buried in a long silence.' Jean de la Fontaine (1621-95), paid to sing the praises of Vaux, wrote *Le Songe de Vaux*, a commission that was not completed. The song adds nothing to either the poet's or the château's renown. 'You know how little I know about architecture,' La Fontaine wrote to his wife, 'and that I said nothing about Vaux except for memories of it.'[15] Molière (1622-73), fulfilled commissions for Foucquet rather than being one of his protégés. *Sganarelle* and *L'Étourdi* were first performed at Saint-Mandé, and one of the first performances of *L'École des maris* was at Vaux. *Les Fâcheux* was commissioned for the last entertainment to be held at Vaux on 17 August 1661.

The eclecticism that is a characteristic of Foucquet's literary patronage means that it is impossible to have a very clear idea of how sound was his artistic judgement. The same is true of his choice of artists and works of art. Anatole France was repeating a commonly held view when he attributed to Foucquet 'the honour of having detected and chosen men of high talent and (having) been the first to employ the great artists of French art whose works created widespread and lasting splendour in the reign of Louis XIV'.[16] But the truth is that Le Vau, Le Brun and Le Nôtre were in the king's service and had already had the opportunity of meeting and indeed working with one another when Foucquet summoned them to Vaux.

Le Vau had been first architect to the king since 1654; Le Brun and Poussin vied for the title of first painter to the king; only Le Nôtre was still awaiting recognition. The same is true of virtually the whole team of painters and sculptors who collaborated on Vaux, even down to his devoted steward Bénigne Courtois who was described as 'major domo ordinary to the king' in 1658. Foucquet certainly dipped deep into the royal staff, whether or not he made liberal use of the state coffers! Almost the only member of staff who seems to have been Foucquet's own find was François Wattel, known as Vatel, 'major domo to Monseigneur the Superintendent', and he is also one of the few members of the Vaux team who did not resurface at Versailles. After fleeing to England Vatel found employment with the Prince of Condé at Chantilly where he sadly achieved fame by committing suicide one day when Condé was entertaining the king. Because the food was too slow in reaching the table Vatel felt that his honour had been compromised. Foucquet's collections included some outstanding pieces – three superb paintings by Paulo Veronese (c. 1528-88) and *La Manne*, one of Nicolas Poussin's (1594-1665) most important paintings – but they do not amount to enough for their owner to be listed as one of the great collectors of the seventeenth century.[17] Like everyone else, Foucquet turned to Italy for his supply of art works, appointing his brother, Abbé Louis Foucquet, to act for him. The Abbé sent his brother very odd advice from Rome.[18] 'When you ask for very good ones [pictures] I do not think you want originals by the world's foremost painters which are amazingly expensive and rare' (28 June 1655). 'I think most of your money should be spent on statues; there can be no question that they embellish large rooms better than wretched pictures the beauty of which few people can appreciate... As I have anticipated that it would be one of your wishes, I am looking only for large pictures suitable for large rooms' (2 August 1655). 'I will look for the best pictures I can from among the mediocre ones you ask me for' (7 March 1656). Obviously the Superintendant was not responsible for the advice he received, but the tone of his brother's letters indicates that he thought it was good. Foucquet commissioned a *Holy Family* from Poussin[19] and one from Le Brun[20]: did he have any other motive than to avail himself of talents that had been highlighted by the admiration evinced for these artists by connoisseurs? The story related by Mariette[21] of Le Brun's drawing depicting the *Rape of the Sabine Women* does not argue in Foucquet's favour. Because Foucquet did not like it Le Brun tore it up, but the sculptor Girardon, recognizing it as a masterpiece, gathered up the pieces and reassembled them. Pierre Puget is regarded as one of Foucquet's finds. In fact it was the financier Girardin who brought him from his provincial home in the south of France. In October 1660 Foucquet sent him to fetch pieces of marble from Genoa. We do not know whether it was a public or a private commission or for what the marble was intended. It is no longer certain that the *Hercule gaulois* in the Louvre was in fact commissioned by Foucquet[22] as had been

Tapestry borders

Drawing by Charles Le Brun. The first drawing with Foucquet's
monogram and emblem was intended for the Maincy tapestry works.
The second is just a repeat of the first,
intended for the Gobelins works, but Louis XIV's motto,
emblem and arms have replaced those of Foucquet.
The *Triumph of Constantine* was woven with borders
made after this drawing.

thought. The commission aroused Colbert's jealousy and he associated Puget with Foucquet's downfall. The two famous groups by Puget, *Milo of Crotona* and *Perseus and Andromeda*, were not accorded a place in the gardens at Versailles until after Colbert's death.

The establishment of the tapestry works at Maincy near the château of Vaux is one of Foucquet's most important initiatives in the field of the arts. From 1658 to 1662 290 people including 19 Flemish tapestry-workers were employed there under Le Brun's supervision. Maincy was elevated to the status of a privileged works for *haute lisse* tapestry by letters of patent from Louis XIV who, with supreme irony, paid tribute to 'the affection and inviolable loyalty' of his Super-intendent.[23] At Colbert's express wish the works continued to function for several months after Foucquet's fall from grace and were then transferred to the Gobelins where the pieces started at Maincy were completed.[24] The establishment of these works demonstrates Foucquet's spirit of enterprise, as does the building of naval docks in Brittany. In this respect, as in financial matters, nobody carried on from where Foucquet left off more faithfully than Colbert himself. To meet the demand for the large quantities of tapestry needed to furnish a modern residence in the

The Triumph of Constantine

Engraving by Audran. Several sets of hangings were started at the Maincy tapestry works near Vaux,
founded by Foucquet, but finished at the Gobelins after Colbert had transferred the tapestry works there.
Among them was the history of Constantine consisting of six tapestries,
three after Raphael and three after Le Brun, including *The Triumph*.
Audran's engraving is a noticeably fuller composition than the one created as a tapestry.

requisite time limits, there was no better solution than to establish a workshop. The kings of France had appreciated this long before Foucquet appeared on the scene, and in the sixteenth century they had tapestries woven for themselves in Paris and at Fontainebleau.

In the final analysis there is only one irrefutable proof to Foucquet's taste – Vaux itself. And it is enough. There are a hundred examples of the huge fortune being spent on the building work, of paintings commissioned by the metre and sculptures charged per item for a masterpiece such as Vaux. Foucquet was not a discoverer of talent, but an astute employer of it. At Vaux everything was of the best.

News of what was going on spread, and the highest nobles in the land asked if they could come and see. Foucquet was reluctant to accede to such requests, whether because he wanted to conceal how much he was spending on Vaux, or because he was saving up for the effect that the finished work was intended to produce. It would in fact have been quite convenient for the receptions and entertainments held between 1659 and 1661 to have been deferred, but curiosity prevailed! On 8

Frieze in the large square room

This frieze, attributed to Charles Le Brun and featuring the squirrel and tower of the Foucquets, must be connected with *The Triumph of Constantine.*
It was no doubt made hurriedly to disguise the fact that the room was unfinished when the entertainments were held in 1661.

February 1657 Foucquet sent Courtois the following note: 'A gentleman living in the vicinity... told the queen that he was recently at Vaux and counted 900 men working on the site. We ought (in order to prevent this as far as possible) to carry out our plan of putting in porters and keeping the doors closed. I would be very pleased if you would push the work on as far as possible before the season when everyone goes to the country and for as few people as can be managed to be seen together.'[25] On 30 May 1657 Vatel wrote to Courtois: 'Monseigneur has indicated that he would very much like to know when M. Colbert was at Vaux... which places he was in and who accompanied him and talked to him during his walk and even what he said.'[26] Two days after being officially received at Vaux, Colbert went back there for a surprise visit, it might be said on a tour of inspection.[27] Another note from Foucquet around June 1659: 'His Eminence [Mazarin] will spend the night at Vaux on Wednesday; the day-workers and masons employed on the Grand Canal should be dismissed so that not many are there; during that time they should be set to work on the farms and at Maincy.'[28] Mazarin did in fact spend the night of 25 June at Vaux on his way to the Pyrenees where he was going to sign the famous peace treaty[29] which, in restoring peace which had so long been absent from the kingdom, possibly proved fatal to Foucquet who had made his fortune in a war economy. A few days later, further instructions from Foucquet: 'The king is going to Fontainebleau in eight or ten days time; remove all evidence of earthworks every-where and let the villagers of Héricy go and harvest grapes as they have requested.'[30] On 14 July Foucquet did entertain the king, the queen mother and Monsieur, the king's brother for a meal. One year later on 10 July he received the king and his young bride Marie-Thérèse for dinner on their return from Saint-Jean-de-Luz where the royal marriage had taken place. This event is reported in Loret's *Muze his-torique*.[31] The following year the *Muze* also mentions the reception arranged for Queen Henrietta Maria of England, Monsieur and Madame; *L'École des maris* was performed on their behalf on 12 July in the chambre des Muses.[32]

Finally the famous final entertainment took place on 17 August 1661, twenty years after the land at Vaux had been purchased. The most detailed account is an anony-mous one: the king arrived from Fontainebleau at 6 p.m. with the court; he rested; he visited the gardens; he had a first meal accompanied by the playing of 24 vio-lins; at the 'grille d'eau' he attended a performance of *Les Fâcheux*, preceded by a homage to the king written by Pellisson; at 1 a.m. he admired fireworks over the canal and as he returned towards the castle a spray of a thousand rockets was released from the dome; another meal, more violins and he returned to Fontainebleau.[33] The most burlesque account is given by Loret whose poetry is

Louis XIV

The history of this replica of the famous bust made by Gianlorenzo Bernini in 1665 has not yet been researched.
This work restores the monarch to his proper place in the Superintendent's residence.

Vaux-le-Vicomte *en fête*

The château and gardens are illuminated every Saturday, conjuring up the splendid entertainment staged by Foucquet for the king on 17 August 1661, marking the official opening of the château and the summit of the Superintendent's career. It is said that Louis XIV, irritated by the lavish display, was tempted to have his Minister arrested at the end of the entertainment. The king and the court left Fontainebleau at 3 p.m. and reached Vaux at 6. The king waited in the apartment set aside for him until the heat of the day had subsided. Then the visit of the gardens commenced; small barouches were made available for the king and queen. They went to the highest point to admire the château from a distance. In the gardens 'there was such a confusion of beautiful things that it cannot be expressed', declared a contemporary who described 'the spurting waters, the canals, the waterfalls, the pathways full of ladies and courtiers decked with ribbons and feathers'. When it grew dark, they went back to the château for a supper prepared by the famous Vatel and accompanied by the music of 24 violins. Then they went to the 'grille d'eau', transformed into an open-air theatre, to attend a performance of Les Fâcheux *by Molière; then at 1 a.m., down to the grand canal for the fireworks. When they were finished it was thought that the entertainment was at an end but as he went back towards the château the king was surprised by 'a thousand rockets' erupting from the dome: 'Lanterns which had been placed close together on the cornice made the building look as if it was ablaze.' A final meal was served to the king who left for Fontainebleau at dawn. La Fontaine has left an account of this entertainment where 'everything vied to please the king: the music, the water display, the lights, the stars'.*

Set for an open-air performance

Drawing by Giacomo Torelli.
It could be the one prepared by this specialist
for set design for the performance of Molière's *Les Fâcheux*
staged at Vaux for the entertainment of 17 August 1661.
The drawing bears the monogram of Louis XIV,
but that replaced Foucquet's on everything
after the Superintendent's downfall,
while the play itself was revived at Versailles in 1664
for the entertainment known as the *Plaisirs de l'Ile enchantée*.

The 'grille d'eau'

This garden construction serving as a pendant to the wrought-iron
railings leading to the vegetable garden owes its name to a row of jets
of water that resemble a grille. It can also serve as the stage for open-air theatre.
It was here that *Les Fâcheux* was first performed.

little better than doggerel: '*Que de dames! Que de mignonnes! / Et que d'adorables per-
sonnes*' (So many ladies! So many pretty ones! / So many delightful people). With
regard to the homage to the king, Loret revels that the '*sage autheur, c'est Pellisson/
Des muzes le vrai nourisson!* (the wise author is Pellisson/ A babe in arms among the
Muses). The most important account is that given by La Fontaine to the Abbé de
Maucroix on 22 August. La Fontaine was well aware of the significance of the event
at which so many famous artists were present.

The outstanding artistic event of the evening was the performance of *Les Fâcheux*.
Not because it is was of Molière's most successful efforts – it was written and learnt
in a fortnight as the author reveals in his prologue. But in the haste a new genre
was born, the *comédie-ballet*, a play incorporating ballet. All seventeenth-century

entertainment included a ballet and a theatrical performance. But as there was only a small number of dancers available at Vaux it occurred to Molière to use the ballet in interludes of the play so as to allow the dancers to change their costumes. Thus there was now 'just one single thing with the ballet and the play' (Molière). The *comédie-ballet* genre was subsequently brilliantly exemplified in collaborations between Molière and Jean-Batiste Lulli.

Was Lulli present at the entertainment? The music for *Les Fâcheux* is believed to have been written by the choreographer Pierre Beauchamps, very famous at the time, and he did supervise the movements of the dancers. As far as we know Beauchamps usually collaborated with Lulli, but did he ever write any music except for *Les Fâcheux*? It would seem that the music is attributed to him only on the basis of an ambiguous comment in Loret's account. Lulli supposedly composed only the *courante* which one of the 'fâcheux' (bores), purporting to be the composer, wants to submit to the judgement of 'Baptiste', i.e. Jean-Baptiste Lulli. Lulli who was as wily as his fellow-countryman Mazarin, had been in the king's service since 1652 and was appointed superintendent of the king's music in 1661. Might he have had a premonition of Foucquet's fall from favour, and avoided compromising himself? [34]

The sets for *Les Fâcheux* were designed by Giacomo Torelli. He had made his name in Paris in 1645, but had a dangerous rival in the person of Gaspare Vigarani whom Mazarin had brought from Italy to build the theatre at the Tuileries.[35] A quarrel between Colbert and Torelli is believed to have had an influence on the selection of Torelli, the last artist Foucquet engaged before being arrested himself. According to the editor of *Les Fâcheux,* one of the sets depicted 'a garden decorated with terms [a tapering pedestal supporting a bust] and several water spouts. You see rocks opening up, terms moving and a naiad emerging from a rock'. It is possible that the 'grille d'eau', a permanent decorative feature, was used for this effect and is thought to have been recognized in a drawing by Torelli.[36] The drawing is marked with a crowned L, not with F for Foucquet. As with the tapestries that went from Maincy to the Gobelins, it is possible that the king's monogram was substituted for that of his Superintendent. What is more, *Les Fâcheux* was revived for the first of the great entertainments staged at Versailles, *Les Plaisirs de l'Île enchantée* (1664).

The authors who have written about Foucquet and Vaux, to paraphrase La Fontaine, have all set about their description of the entertainment; and they all hurried to desert the château and rush to Nantes. There on the king's orders, Foucquet was arrested on 5 September by D'Artagnan, an officer in the musketeers. At this late date, were people still busy in the galleries of the great building abandoned by the Viceroy of the West Indies?

Jacques de Beaune Semblençay, executed on the orders of Francis I in 1527, is less well known, but with all due respect to Morand his sentence had already aroused the partisan sympathy of poets, of Clément Marot in particular.[46]

The similarity between the fates of all these men prompts a general explanation of the case illustrated by the building of Vaux. Office-holders were the main promoters of French architecture, and in particular they were prolific builders of châteaux. The château like the office itself was a means of achieving the ennoblement towards which these bourgeois families in pursuit of social success aspired. The before and after scenarios of the Coeur and the Foucquet families are identical. 'Every bourgeois wants to build like the great lords,' La Fontaine wrote in the fable *La grenouille qui voulait se faire aussi grosse que le boeuf* [The frog that wanted to be as big as the ox]. And things that are blown up sometimes burst! The buildings of Coeur and Foucquet are not scandalous in themselves: they are scandalous only through lack of deference for the king who no longer occupies the place due to him. The circumstances, a civil war and a foreign war, explained Charles VII's reticence in dealing with the situation, as well as that of Louis XIII and of Louis XIV in his early youth. Financiers' schemes proliferated in this vacuum. The same causes produced the same effects. René de Longueil, a parliamentarian who played an ambiguous role during the Fronde but was nonetheless appointed Superintendent of Finance in 1650, built the château of Maisons, entertained the king there, and was disgraced. For the king to resume his rightful place in his own kingdom this situation had to stop. No doubt an important change in the political and architectural scheme of things dates from the fall of Foucquet. When we think about it, the bastions built at Belle-Isle for Foucquet were the last private fortification works carried out in France! With the advent of Vauban the only fortresses to be built were on the frontiers and for the king.

Foucquet's end

At certain hours on certain days in certain seasons,
the château seems gradually to recover the splendour
with which it was imbued by the entertainment of 17 August 1661:
the clouds gather above it as if at the approach of the tragic storm that followed the entertainment;
the water and woods are veiled as if to don mourning for the unfortunate Superintendent.

Following pages

The drawbridge crossing the moat between the main building and the gardens.
The whole castle, seen from the gardens, the square pool in the foreground.

The buildings

Sequence of proposals • Chronology of the work • Le Vau's collaborators
General approach • Internal layout • Façades • Outbuildings

Vaux is mentioned in all the guidebooks, collections, memoirs and historical studies as one of the most remarkable châteaux in the Ile-de-France, which in effect means anywhere in France. Its reputation is to a large extent based on its gardens and interior decorative scheme. Nonetheless one cannot fail to marvel when first discovering the huge mass of the building. A detailed study does not destroy this first impression, quite the opposite. Perhaps it would be easier to write the history of the château of Vaux if the documentation on it were less extensive: the evidence of contemporaries is contradictory; the various inventories and minutes drawn up for Foucquet's trial and sentence, partial in both senses of the word, create a tiresome illusion of being exhaustive. Moreover, for different reasons judges and historians alike have had a shared interest in mistakenly cutting down the time spent on designing and creating this masterpiece: the judges to justify their accusation of peculation, and historians so that the feats of 'Nicolas the Magnificent' can be exalted.

Where the construction is concerned two schemes have been preserved, one a drawing which looks exactly like working plans, and the other an engraving, which is taken to be the scheme as it was carried out. Both, however, differ from the building as it stands. On the verso of the drawing is the note: 'Initialled in its final form, to be carried out following the decision made this second day of

The moats

The outbuildings in the background.

Scheme by Louis Le Vau, 1656

Louis Le Vau,
first architect to the king,
may have been working on the site
for some time when he signed this scheme
which was carried out with some alterations,
the most important being the substitution
of course work made entirely of ashlars
for the brick and stone course work
in the scheme.
On the reverse of the courtyard elevation
it bears the dates 2 and 10 August 1656
and the signatures of Foucquet,
Le Vau and the building contractor Villedo.

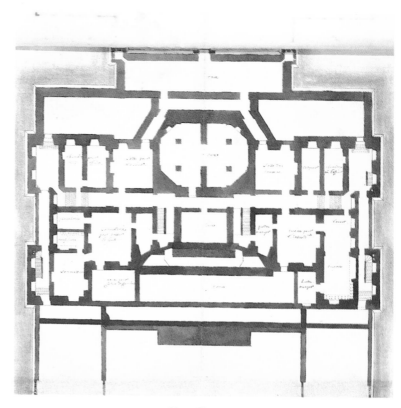

Plan of basement

Courtyard elevation

seen] through these three openings.'[20] The vestibule at the château of Maisons which may have served as a model for Vaux also went from one side of the building to the other, and was enclosed only by railings. A comparable arrangement crops up again in Le Vau's first scheme for Versailles. These spaces which were exposed to the winds and appear so incongruous to our cold-fearing century were common, not only in Italy, but also in France, where stairs in particular often had only openings with no frames, like the staircase at the Hôtel Lambert, also designed by Le Vau.

Thus at Vaux the vestibule-salon block formed such a powerful central section that the layout of the two sides is organized almost independently, each with its own staircase. We observe the symmetry of the two large apartments overlooking the garden, both formed of a suite consisting of an antechamber, a main room and a study, the typical make-up of the French apartment since the mid-sixteenth century. The antechamber, known as a 'chambre', though it was a reception room, had even been invented in the previous century; people waited there before being received in the main room. In the eighteenth century when the word 'salon' was finally established to describe the main reception room, the term 'chambre à coucher' would be used. At Vaux Foucquet's bedroom was in fact upstairs.

The study or 'cabinet' was derived from the piece of furniture with secret drawers in which the most important papers were kept: the master of the house retired to it to work or to receive someone in private. The apartment on the left was the king's apartment; [21] the one on the right was the Superintendent's state apartment.[22] It is not surprising that there was an apartment which would be used only in the event of a possible visit by the king. It was traditional, and all the more justified because until the end of the century the kings of France led a virtually nomadic existence. Every distinguished château had at least one king's room, which, for most of the time, was unoccupied. But at Vaux the symmetry of the two apartments illustrates the role of a double main building which has a long history in France.[23] It can in fact be found at Maisons where René de Longueil, a precursor of Foucquet both as a parliamentarian and as superintendent, had an apartment that was a symmetrical counterpart of the king's on the first floor. It

Central salon

(Double page over)
The openings on to the garden, originally with no joinery work,
were closed off only by wrought-iron railings.
The vestibule, which also had no wooden frames, formed a covered
but unenclosed passageway between the courtyard and the garden.

occurs again in Antoine Le Pautre's château where, as we understand it, Mazarin's apartment would have been a counterpart of the king's. The symmetry of the two meanings of the word *hôte* in French (host or guest) no doubt justified an equality otherwise so at variance with etiquette.

The purpose of the rooms on the courtyard side was obviously not finally fixed when the Superintendent fell from power. On the drawing these rooms complement the grand apartments. The antechambers on the garden side also give access to the rooms on the courtyard side; there are baths on the left which can also be found on the engraved design. The latter gives no indication of the function of the rooms on the courtyard side. In the inventories the large right-hand room is referred to as a 'large square room', but the matching left-hand room is described as a 'dining-room'. It was in the mid-seventeenth century that people started to set a room aside for meals which up until then had been taken at occasional tables in the antechambers. At the same time a change occurred in the use of china and cutlery. Foucquet would certainly have eaten his meat with a fork without fearing the accusation of depravity still associated with that practice a few years earlier. According to the trial Foucquet owned 'five hundred dozen' plates and a service in solid gold, 'and the king does not have one !' (it was more probably silver-gilt). The fact that the left-hand room was intended as a dining-room is confirmed by the small room adjoining it being referred to as a 'buffet' (serving area) in the inventories. The dining-room and its symmetrical counterpart are the only rooms on the ground floor with vaulted ceilings – the vaulting ensured that the room would remain relatively cool.

To sum up, we have to concede that Le Vau did not really manage to take proper advantage of the fine invention of a double block. He ended up with a traditional sequence of two apartments on the garden side, while he did not know what to do with rooms on the courtyard side ! We notice that there is no library although Foucquet was a great lover of books. His library (14,000 of his books were bought for the king's library after the dispersal of his property) was at Saint-Mandé. A library was not installed in the king's antechamber until the eighteenth century.

The scheme in the drawing includes a ground plan of the basement with its layout. The basement extends below the terrace on the courtyard side where it includes a drain which collected waste water from the main building. It has a longitudinal corridor, numerous service rooms, a kitchen, cellars, pantries and even rooms for the household officials, (i.e. those in charge of ensuring service). The kitchen is on the other side from the dining-room, but it did communicate with the serving-area by means of the longitudinal corridor and the left-hand stair.

The style of Le Vau's architecture does not follow the straight line of French tradition, which led to him being criticized by the advocates of Classicism who saw François Mansart, Le Vau's rival, as their champion. And yet the subtle interplay of the rustication, the projections, the tablets and the overall outline and proportions which characterizes the façades of Vaux is quintessentially French. But this interplay is disrupted by the mediocre quality of the course work, although it is a technique in which the French excelled. Did Le Vau dispense with the collaboration of a foreman mason, or is this the result of the haste with which building work was carried out? There is no link between the cutting of the dressed stone and the design of the mouldings. What is more, the transition between the sandstone used in the lower parts of the building and the limestone in the upper parts is not cleanly made. All this leads us to surmise that the intention was to re-point it with a coat of stone-like paint, and observations made during a recent restoration seem to confirm this.

The outbuildings are mainly built of brick and stone, as we have said. But if we look more closely the hierarchy of the materials is more subtle. The buildings that are nearest the front are in rendered quarry stone, in the style of peasant buildings in the Ile-de-France. The gradation is so organized that the middle buildings have one façade built in brick and stone, and the other in rendered quarry stone. The slope of the roof corresponding to the first façade is covered in slates, while that corresponding to the second is covered in flat tiles. Thus the red, white and black livery marks out the building for servants who were not to be confused with the master's peasants.[28] According to the mason questioned during the trial, the slopes of the roofs at Saint-Mandé were covered with slate on the side which people saw on arriving, and with tiles at the back, (i.e. on the Vincennes side).[29] This was maliciously interpreted as proof of the duplicity of the Superintendent who supposedly used tiles, a less noble and expensive material than slate, on the side facing Mazarin's residence to conceal the scale of his expenditure. Obviously no contemporary made a sincere mistake in interpreting this. Morand who probably thought slates and tiles were equally expensive goes one better than the mason: he writes that at the house at Saint-Mandé the roofs were thatched 'on the side the king could see, and made of tiles on the side that could not be seen'.[30]

The contemporary drawings are too sketchy to describe how the outbuildings were organized. The precise enumeration of the buildings by the roofer Alexandre Girard, who undertook to maintain the roofing on 23 March 1661,[31] can be

The outbuildings seen from the moat

Centrally placed in the background
is one of the mock gates.

Elevation of the outbuildings overlooking the forecourt

Both of these figures show one end
of this elevation, on the side of the chapel courtyard.
We see clearly that the large pavilion
with the mansard roof and the large gate in the same
design have been introduced to complement
the more modestly handled central part.

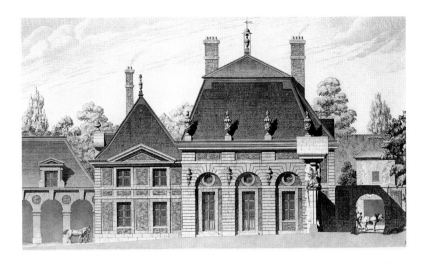

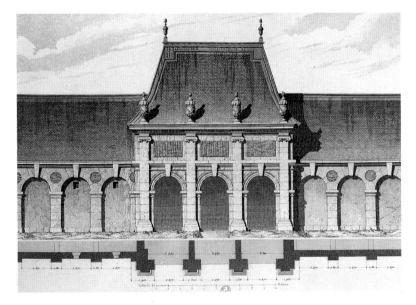

Sections of the stable courtyard

Detailed drawing by Rudolf Pfnor, 1888.
Above : the large pavilion
with a mansard roof can be seen between
the stable courtyard and the farmyard.
Below : the wing and pavilion forming
the garden side of the stable courtyard.

Outbuildings

The buildings for those in service are built of brick
and stone and roofed with slates.
The farm is built of rendered quarry stones
and roofed with tiles. The blocks between the servants'
quarters and the farm are roofed with slates on one
side, and tiles on the other.

related to a detailed plan dating from 1740. The buildings are laid out in two symmetrical groups on either side of a forecourt made of beaten earth.[32] Each half includes a large, enclosed courtyard, called the chapel courtyard on the left and the stables courtyard on the right, and a yard. The main courtyards are bounded by two lines of long buildings and pavilions. The left-hand courtyard was originally enclosed by a building of which only the chapel remains. A similar layout had been intended with an audience chamber symmetrically matching the chapel, a room that had not yet been built when the Superintendent who would have held audience there fell from power. On the other hand the section at the back of that courtyard was built on the right-hand side, but not until the nineteenth century, at the same time as the ruins of the block on the left were razed. The 1740 plan describes the purpose of the buildings: lodgings, stables, barns, workshops. The pavilions contained the apartments assigned to the most important members of staff (the chaplain, steward etc). On the left we can see a dovecote, now gone. According to the same plan the two 'peasant' yards were farmyards. In particular we may note the barn with its large porch, traditional in the region. But according to the contract with the roofer, while the left-hand courtyard was a farm, the one on the right was a menagerie: therefore the Superintendent envisaged housing some animals to provide amusement.

A start may have been made on constructing the outbuildings before the main building was under way, but they were not completed in 1661. The roofer's contract includes 'the audience chamber which is to be made in the yard on the right hand side as you go in, as a symmetrical counterpart of the said chapel' and the 'two pavilions which are to be made in the forecourt following the drawing'. These are obviously the two large pavilions which already appear in the view shown by Israël Silvestre. These two pavilions, more noble in style and actually featuring mansard roofs, are not completely contemporary with the other outbuildings. To counterbalance them, monumental gates with three arches evocative of a triumphal arch were also added on the garden side.

The large railings enclosing the forecourt do not yet appear on Silvestre's view. Madeleine de Scudéry whose description is based on Silvestre's engravings does not mention it. Yet the metalworker Claude Venard had iron delivered for the

The railings

(Double page over)

External view

Mock gate

Detailed drawing by Rudolf Pfnor, 1888.
The railings consist of a series of posts in the form of terms,
with a face sculpted on either side,
wrought-iron rails and two mock gates.

Interior view

In the foreground is the gateway of the main courtyard

View of one of the mock gates

'balustrade of the forecourt'[33] in June 1660, and in March 1661 he had carried out 'the overthrow for the forecourt above the main gate which is 12 feet wide with two large brackets of square iron turned with a double scroll, six-foot-high ornaments forming a large bouquet in the middle fitted with finials and two other bouquets on the two sides with the same embellishments'. The large terms which punctuate the iron railings have remained rough hewn, indicating that the work was not completed.

This great stone and iron structure enclosing the château is an important construction in several respects. The enclosure of Vaux comes at the end of a two-century-long development which led to the view being opened up along the axis of the château – it had previously been blocked by mediaeval buildings and at the beginning of the century was still encumbered by a large stone gateway. The decisive innovation occurred at Maisons where Mansart made a double gate, placing between the two doorways a ditch which closed off the courtyard without blocking the view. Le Vau remembered that ingenious solution, and planned two side gateways made of stone (they are artificial – unless it was originally intended that they should be opening gates). But Vaux stands out because of the extent of the railings, and this solution would be adopted in all French châteaux from the mid-seventeenth century, following the example of Vaux.

Railings between the main gardens and the kitchen garden

The rustic genre, typified here by the use of rustication and of sandstone alternating with limestone, is evocative of the kitchen garden, itself rustic in nature.

Right : Detailed drawing by Rudolf Pfnor, 1888.

The mechanization of iron cutting resulted in a considerable development of the use of metal in architecture in the space of 50 years, particularly for large items such as stair or balcony balustrades or for railings used as an enclosure. *La Fidelle ouverture de l'art de la serrurerie* (La Flèche, 1627) by Mathurin Jousse, the first book published on the subject, shows only small items, locks, knockers and fittings. In *Le Livre d'architecture* by Alexandre Francine (1631) there is a wrought iron gate. These became larger c.1640 at the château of Carrouges in Normandy where there were forges belonging to the lord of the house. Even so, the place occupied by ironwork at Vaux was unprecedented. Hanicle provided the stair balustrades, Venard the railings for the entrance gate, the false monumental gates with their three arches, the vestibule and salon doors and the vegetable garden gate. Forges were established at Maincy to supply the needs of the château. Was this merely the result of fashion, or did it have something to do with the fact that Le Vau himself was an ironmaster? He had bought the forge of Glisolles in Normandy in 1650. It is true that it specialized in manufacturing tinplate, the use of which in sheet form in buildings was rivalled only by lead. But might he not also have had some foundry which would have benefited from the Superintendent's orders?[34]

The attribution of the gardens of Vaux to André Le Nôtre who was living in the château at the time of the sale in 1661 must be reconsidered in view of a garden site that had been under preparation for a long time. Vaux is commonly given as the great gardener's first important achievement, and we may justifiably feel surprise at the age of this beginner: 48 years old in 1661! Had he been at Vaux for long? According to 'the summary of André Le Nôtre's life' published in 1730 and attributed to his nephew Claude Desgots, Le Nôtre 'was nearly 40 when M. Foucquet gave him the opportunity to make his name through the magnificent gardens of Vaux-le-Vicomte'.[4] That would mean that Le Nôtre arrived at Vaux c.1653, a year which has already been widely referred to when Foucquet was appointed Superintendent. In *Le Siècle de Louis XIV* (1751) Voltaire writes that these gardens 'considered the most beautiful in Europe' were 'partly (our underlining) planted by Le Nôtre'. The main guides of the area round Paris which mention the role of Le Brun and Le Vau give long descriptions of the gardens at Vaux without attributing them to Le Nôtre, though tribute is paid to him in many a passage as 'an unparalleled genius', but in connection with other places. It is true that as guides copy from each other one slip of the pen may lie behind this surprising unanimity.[5] Le Nôtre must nonetheless have worked at Vaux for more than ten years, arriving in good time to deal with the generous enlargement of the estate resulting from the purchase of the Vaux pond in 1656. From 1643 if not before André Le Nôtre bore the title of 'designer of the plants and beds of all His Majesty's gardens', and from 1657 if not earlier that of 'comptroller general of the buildings, gardens, tapestry works and workshops of France'. On 14 September 1661, the day before the inventory of his lodgings at Vaux was made, he attended his daughter's christening with the title of 'adviser to the king and comptroller general of his buildings and gardens'. Were these titles due to a long period of patronage by Foucquet or were they merely the culmination of the good fortune of three generations of Le Nôtres who had served the king? For all these fine-sounding titles the first major work with which his name is associated is Vaux. If he worked on the garden of the Tuileries palace like his father and grandfather before him, he did nothing decisive there until Colbert commissioned him to open up the Champs Élysées avenue in 1668.[6]

We should perhaps look among those who taught André Le Nôtre for the person who preceded him at Vaux. Obviously we must discount the painter Simon Vouet (1590-1649) in whose studio, according to Guillet de Saint-Georges, he learnt to draw and met Le Brun. His father Jean Le Nôtre is a possible candidate. In 1629 he collaborated with Le Mercier at the château of Richelieu where the gardens foreshadow those of Vaux. He was still alive in 1658; the exact date of his death is not known. The Mollets and the Le Nôtres worked together on the Tuileries garden for several generations. In 1630 Claude II bought the surviving interest of his father Jacques as gardener at the Tuileries. A letter of patent dated 27 February 1632 appointed him 'gardener in ordinary and designer of plants, parks and gardens for the royal houses', and this patent was confirmed on 25 June 1643. André Le Nôtre took over from him at the Tuileries, so why not at Vaux? Yet if Claude II Mollet had been responsible for the initial work at Vaux, would the publisher of his treatise not have mentioned this in his dedication to Foucquet?

If we look through the names of those who collaborated with Le Nôtre at Vaux, we find no possible rival: Antoine Trumel, a gardener, Claude Robillard, a fountain-maker. Jean de La Quintinie who created the kitchen garden at Versailles, the author of *Instructions pour les jardins fruitiers et potagers avec un traité des orangers* (published posthumously, 1690), is the only one to have achieved fame, but there is no proof that he laid out the kitchen garden at Vaux. After going to Italy as a mentor to the son of President Tambonneau, he created the garden of Le Vau's Hôtel Tambonneau (1641). General biographical dictionaries say he played a part at Vaux, except for Charles Perrault's *Hommes illustres qui ont paru en France pendant le XVIIᵉ siècle* (1696). What is the origin of this opinion shared by a number of those who have written about Foucquet and Vaux,[7] too widely expressed for us to be able to discount it once and for all?

The large *Plan du chasteau de Vaux-le-Vicomte de M. Foucquet* held at the Institut,[8] an exceptional exhibit in the history of the French garden, certainly post-dates the purchase in 1656, but perhaps not by far because the plans of the buildings have not yet been finally settled. It can be identified as the working plan established on Le Nôtre's arrival, but drawn by a collaborator, possibly Pierre Desgots, Le Nôtre's brother-in-law and the father of Claude Desgots.[9] The *Livre de plans de la seigneurie de Moisenay faisant partie de la duché-pairie de Villars* which gives an account of the state of the gardens and park in 1740 illustrates that this scheme was carried out virtually to the letter.

The series of 'views' drawn and engraved by Israël Silvestre is the first source of information about the gardens at Vaux.[10] It was shown to Christian Huygens, the famous Dutch scholar, on his journey to France in 1660. In his diary for 16 December he notes: 'Saw Israël Silvestre who showed me his drawings and plates

VEVE ET PERSPECTIVE DV CHASTEAV DE VAVX, PAR LE COSTÉ

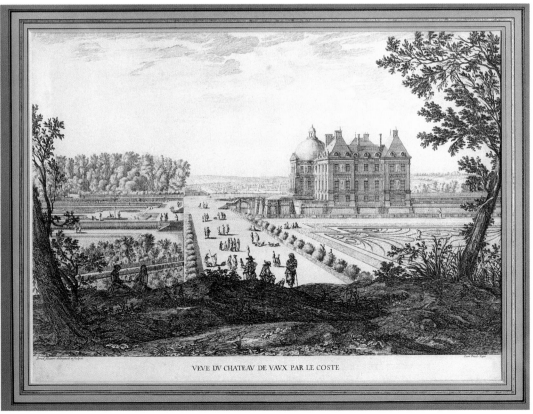

VEVE DV CHATEAV DE VAVX PAR LE COSTE

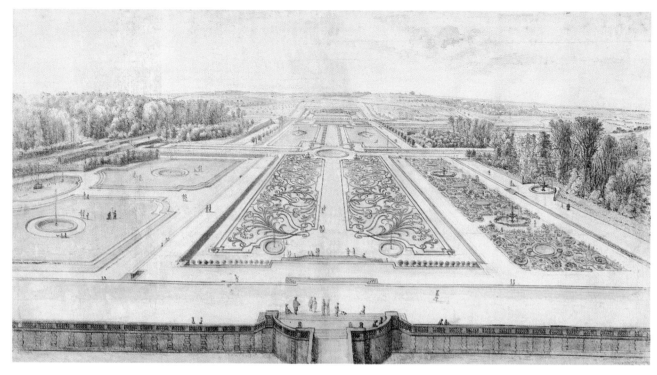

View of the garden from the château

Drawing by Israël Silvestre. In the centre the *parterres de broderie*;
on the right the flowerbed; on the left the *parterre de la Couronne.*

View of the parterre de la Couronne

Engraving by Israël Silvestre.

View of the Fontaine de la Couronne

Engraving by Israël Silvestre.

View of the flowerbed

Drawing by Israël Silvestre. The main building has not yet been built.
Its site is occupied by a mound of earth.

View from the parterre de la Couronne

Engraving by Israël Silvestre.

The parterres de broderie

(Double page over)
In the foreground, the *parterres de broderie*,
in the background the grotto
which is separated from the first part
of the gardens by the canal:
the canal only becomes obvious once
we reach its edge.

View of the 'grille d'eau'

Engraving by Israël Silvestre.
Several differences can be observed
between the engraving
and the photograph,
apart from the fact that
in the engraving there is a grille
formed from water.
Two human figures are on the site
occupied by the two dogs.
In the upper part, however,
the two sheathed figures recur.

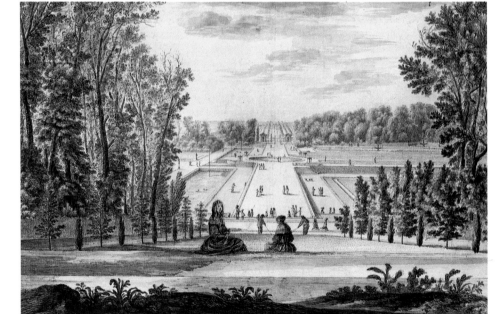

View from the 'grille d'eau'

Engraving by Israël Silvestre.

Side view of the 'grille d'eau'

Drawing by Israël Silvestre.
The château is in the distance.

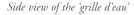

View of the 'grille d'eau'

VEVE EN PERSPECTIVE DES CASCADES DE VAVX

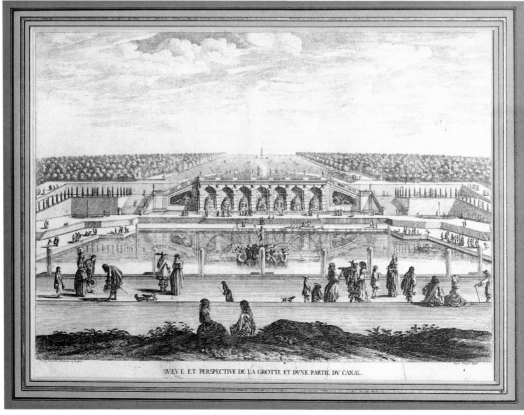

VEVE ET PERSPECTIVE DE LA GROTTE ET D'VNE PARTIE DV CANAL.

View of the waterfalls

Engraving by Israël Silvestre.
In the background on the left
a sort of loggia nicknamed the confessional
(in the nineteenth century).

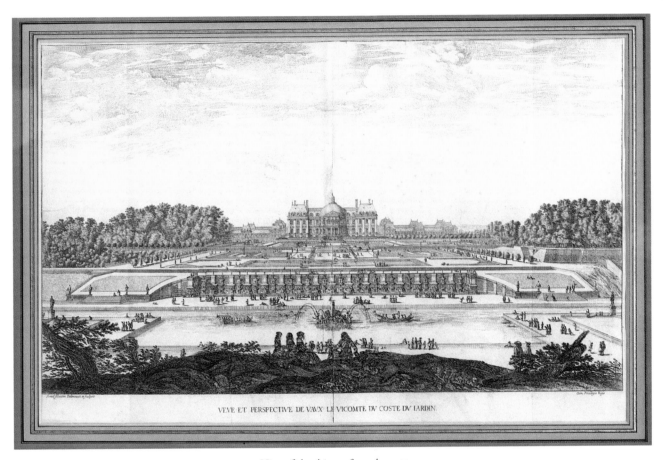

VEVE ET PERSPECTIVE DE VAVX LE VICOMTE DV COSTE DV IARDIN.

View of the château from the grotto

Engraving by Israël Silvestre. In the middle distance are the waterfalls.

View of the grotto from the waterfalls

Engraving by Israël Silvestre.
In the middle of the pool is a Neptune
(no longer there) and in the distance the statue of Hercules,
which was not installed until the nineteenth century.

current state is a twentieth-century invention.[14] The second zone is made up of three parterres enclosed by box-edges – *parterres de broderie* – lying between the *parterre de la couronne* on the left and the *parterre des fleurs* on the right. Each of these side beds contains three fountains: the middle fountain on the left is decorated with the crown which gives that bed its name. The gardens on the right foreshadowed the Trianon gardens which were entirely devoted to flowers. Like the king Foucquet was a great lover of flowers – they were *grippés de fleurs* to use the expression current at the time. Anemones, tulips and tuberoses were in fashion.[15] Among the gardeners at Vaux it was the florist who received the best treatment from Foucquet, although, as his contemporaries noted, he was a German and a Lutheran!

The second zone is separated from the third by a sizeable transversal axis formed by a pathway and a small canal with a round pool in the middle, the *rondeau*. 'Around the rondeau are four little Cupids holding shells on their heads from which we see water constantly spilling over... and falling on to small squares of turf.'[16] These are the first examples of those little putti who were to proliferate at Versailles. The right end of this transversal axis leads to the wrought-iron gate leading into the vegetable garden – the iron for this was delivered by the metal-worker Claude Venard in August 1661;[17] the left end leads to the small waterfalls, also known as the 'grille d'eau'. 'Quite far away you see a wrought-iron gate leading into a rustic orchard and on the left on rising ground going between the woods a waterfall over turf, representing a sort of grille of water relating to the real grille which is on the other side.'[18]

The third zone is divided into two by a longitudinal waterway which is lined with water spouts producing the effect of a 'crystal balustrade'; at the end of the water-way there is a 'square of water' while on either side of it are two beds with a rounded pond. On the left of the square pool stands a sort of loggia or grotto, and straight ahead of it there is a transversal pathway which might well mark the end of the original gardens. Right across these three zones the vegetable gardens and wooded groves run along the sides of the fountains and beds.[19] According to a maintenance contract dated 1697 the trees were to be cut to form hedgerows. The species are elm, lime, sweet chestnut, chestnut, hornbeam, fir, cherry, laurel and box.[20] From the entrance down to the square pool the gardens with their side cover and open centre form a coherent whole. However there is nothing that would suggest that they were finished before Le Nôtre's arrival. Lines by Pellisson explicitly credit Le Nôtre with the invention of the crown and the four cupids, and a sort of overall control of the gardens as a whole.[21] As far as the crown and cupids are concerned we are readily inclined to recognize Le Nôtre as their creator because they crop up again at Versailles.

From the square pool onwards the composition changes in scale and unquestionably bears the stamp of Le Nôtre. The square pool is the hook attaching the second gardens to the first gardens. By a carefully studied optical effect, the pool, when seen from the château, appears to be part of a grotto which in fact stands beyond the canal.[22] The canal is one kilometre long, at the head of which is a round pool known as the *poêle* (frying pan). On the main axis of the gardens the canal swells out to form a rectangular pool, 'an abyss of water, if it must be so said'. On the near side the waterfalls are formed on the sloping ground, with two rows of water spouts and 'four long rows of shells full of water spilling over into one another'; and on the far side stands the grotto, the most famous garden building at Vaux. It is attributed to Le Nôtre by the caption on an Silvestre-Pérelle print published by Langlois, and to Méléandre (i.e. Le Brun) in *Clélie*. With regard to the decoration of the rectangular pool the evidence of Madeleine de Scudéry and Silvestre differs. Above the grotto Silvestre mentions the 'gerbe', a water spout spraying water 5 meters high, which Madeleine de Scudéry describes as a 'large crystal column'.

The large figure of Hercules which today rounds off the composition is a nineteenth-century sculpture, and does not appear on the 1740 plan. But it was certainly proposed in Foucquet's day. In the distance in Silvestre's print is the silhouette of the *Farnese Hercules*, the famous antique statue of the hero at rest, leaning on his club. Madeleine de Scudéry explains the meaning of the figure: 'As if to show that it is the final piece of this great and beautiful work, they have put... a fine figure of Hercules resting after all his labours which can be seen depicted in low relief on the plinth.'[23] The Hercules resting after completing the huge labour the garden represents is no doubt Foucquet himself, depicted several times in the guise of the antique hero in the paintings in the château.[24] But the Hercules of Vaux did not have time to turn back and contemplate his finished labour, and if he found rest, rest for the body if not for the soul, it was far away from Vaux.

The plans and contemporary accounts mentioned other projects which like the Hercules in Foucquet's time came to nothing, and about which even less is known. The strangest are the 'two pyramids in imitation of those near Memphis' which Méléandre wanted to have built 'in a rather irregular little corner of earth' to house the two Egyptian mummies Foucquet had in his collection.[25] It may be conjectured that if they had been built they would have had an impact on the history of the French garden.

Children and seahorses

This sculpted group, commissioned from
Alfred Lanson by Alfred Sommier in the 1880s,
is on the same level as the square pool. In the distance,
beyond the canal, is the grotto.

The torrent

Outlet of the system of underground
conduits into the canal.

The canal

The river Anqueil, channelled into a canal,
forms the main transversal axis.

That history which more or less merges with the history of the French château was slow to reach fruition. The mediaeval *hortus conclusus*, independant of the house, is closed like a flower in bud. The seventeenth-century French garden is a stream gushing through the middle of the house, removing the woodland in its passage and projecting itself towards a fixed point far away in the countryside. At one fell swoop it gave the measure of the estate. Even the dovecote was like a large abacus painstakingly counting off the acreage – each pigeonhole representing an arpent (roughly an acre).

At Vaux this development is completed. But was this not already the case in the great gardens of the first half of the seventeenth century, particularly those created for Cardinal Richelieu, the protector of Foucquet's father and Nicolas's model? At Richelieu where the hierarchy of the courtyards and forecourts, the main building and the outbuildings was carefully regulated, the widening of the central pathway, its development into a Y-junction, the clear distinction between what was covered and what was open and the canalization of a river were all things that foreshadowed Vaux. Even the large number of statues, as we will see, was also characteristic of Vaux.

Among the signs of modernity, the importance of which becomes evident only on analysis, was the *parterre de broderie*. Two practical gardeners and gardening theorists claimed to have virtually invented it: Jacques Boyceau de La Barauderie and Claude II Mollet. In the posthumous edition of the *Traité de jardinage* (1638), Boyceau and his nephew Jacques de Menours are given as the creators of the *parterres de broderie* at the Luxembourg palace and Louis XIII's Versailles, several decades ahead of Vaux, while Mollet in his treatise claims to have learnt how to create such parterres with his father who while collaborating with Dupérac, had created the parterres at Anet at the end of the sixteenth century: 'They are the first parterres and compartments *de broderie* to have been made in France,' Mollet writes. At first glance it is hard to see what distinguishes such a parterre from the chequerboard box-edged squares of garden found in the Renaissance period, full of patterns that might have been copied from *La fleur de la science de portraicture et patrons de broderie façon arabicque et italique* by Francisque Pelegrin (1525), although this 'book of foliage, intertwined patterns and Moorish and Damascene works' was not specifically addressed to gardeners. In his *Thresor des parterres de l'univers* (Geneva, 1629) Loris sketches out a typology of bedding, in which the *figures à la française* are interwoven in such a way that the paths crisscross like lakes of love or other things that become entangled' – leaving us all the wiser! Mollet however makes the implications of this invention perfectly clear:

Views of the grotto

This garden structure
is the most famous at Vaux:
people came from all over Europe to see it
and it was widely copied.
Whether it was designed by Le Nôtre
or Le Brun is not known.

The Nile

Freely inspired by the famous antique group,
the Nile at the end of the gardens conjures up
the Roman references that are omnipresent at Vaux.

View of the grotto from the upper flight of stairs

At the bottom of the stairs we can see two lions holding
a horn of plenty and the Foucquet squirrel.

The Anqueil

The use of the Anqueil, the small river Le Nôtre exploited to form the canal,
as a pendant to the Nile can be interpreted as French art challenging Roman art.

Atlas

The treatment of atlantes is borrowed
from Italian garden art: the model may be
the 'grotte des pins' at Fontainebleau,
made by Italians working for Francis I.

Right-hand side of the grotto

'Forty or fifty years ago [i.e. at the beginning of the century] there were only small compartments in each garden square with various types of pattern.' Instead there was now just one 'single garden' made up of a 'single compartment divided in half by large paths'.[26] It is in fact possible to identify the two parterres with their generous interweaving patterns that develop symmetrically in relation to the central path as a single compartment.

The invention of the *parterre de broderie* therefore forms part of the major task of unifying the garden which was completed in the work of François Mansart at Balleroy, Petit-Bourg, Fresnes and Maisons by the central opening. Christian Huygens saw those gardens during his first journey to France in 1655.[27] At Fresnes, he writes, 'you enter a path sixty feet wide which at the far end looks out over very beautiful countryside'. At Maisons the ha-ha in the forecourt was created in front of the main building 'so as not to impede the view of a wide and beautiful avenue stretching as far as the eye can see'. Biographers have very hesitantly put forward Mansart's name among others as the master who taught Le Nôtre architecture as a young man. It seems to us that the 'short account of the buildings', biographical notes on Jules Hardouin-Mansart written by one of his collaborators c.1690,[28] removes all doubt. It was actually written during Le Nôtre's lifetime saying that François Mansart, Jules Hardouin's uncle, had given him 'openings': Mansart 'was all the more pleased to do so because he found him [Le Nôtre] a person worthy of benefiting from them and, whatever merits M. Le Nôtre may have, he cannot refuse making this acknowledgement to the infinite merits of the late M. Mansart'. The two men may have worked together at the château of Blois, as Le Nôtre had been 'gardener to Monsieur the king's brother' (references in 1635, 1640, 1642).

We may conjecture that the gardens at Vaux were firstly the work of Mollet and secondly in the style of Mansart, but the whole achievement as far as posterity is concerned is by Le Nôtre and *à la française*. If they are quoted as the earliest gardens *à la française* this is because at Vaux there was the first awareness that an original 'national' art form had been created. But the invention cannot be attributed to Le Nôtre. In 1600 Olivier de Serres in his famous *Théâtre d'agriculture* composed the subsequently tirelessly repeated refrain vaunting the superiority of the French garden over the Italian one. As for Le Nôtre himself, when he went to Italy he did not see any garden that made the journey worthwhile!

Winter

This figure is one of several sculptures in the garden whose origin has not been determined. Its identification as Winter is itself tentative.

The 'Gerbe'

The distinguishing feature of this fountain used to be a jet of water
rising to a height of over three metres.

Pool in the beds bordering the waterway path

The pools in the beds which used to be separated by the waterway
(which has not been reinstated) are embellished with a group consisting
of a Triton and a child (in the foreground) and a group with a naiad
and a child (in the background) by Émile Peynot (1888-89).

View taken from above the grotto

(Double page over)

The gardens at Vaux were the nursery for those at Versailles, the masterpiece of the genre: it was the propagator of adult talents, new ideas and young shoots. In July 1665 when the gardener Antoine Trumel was taken on at Versailles he transported several shrubs there. In December another 1,250 standing trees followed, and a final transfer took place in 1668.[29] Among these saplings were orange trees which were immediately placed under cover in the orangery which Le Vau had built at Versailles. Orange trees were in fashion,[30] they were Louis XIV's favourite species. There was no important residence that did not have its orangery, and there was one at Vaux.[31] According to his brother the Abbé Foucquet had sent for 'slips of the rarest orange and lemon trees from Italy, taken from the most famous gardens in Rome'. In 1661 a small gardening manual conveniently appeared teaching 'the manner of planting, cultivating and raising all sorts of trees': it was still dedicated to Foucquet and bore the title *Jardin royal.*[32] That same year Louis XIV regained the exclusive right to use the word 'royal'.

The canal

The children and seahorses sculpted by Alfred Lanson (1880)
stand above the waterfall.

The decorative scheme

The role of Le Brun • Other artists
The salon • The chambre des Muses • The cabinet des jeux • The salon d'Hercule
The king's apartment • The rooms overlooking the courtyard
The upstairs apartments • Sculptures on the façades • Sculptures in the gardens

Méléandre, the 'dark man' in *Clélie*, alias Charles 'Le Brun' (a pun on his name), the third protagonist on the building site at Vaux, created for Foucquet one of the most remarkable decorative schemes of the seventeenth century, which would serve as a model at Versailles until Le Brun's fall from favour. He made a late appearance on the scene at Vaux, coming in the autumn of 1658,[1] i.e. at the point when the major building work had been carried out and the painter was awaited. He had already painted several pictures for Foucquet, though apparently not before 1655.[2] Moreover he was not on the Superintendent's pension list; his stay in Italy (1642-45) had been financed by Chancellor Séguier, an enemy of Foucquet. Le Brun was apparently in the king's service from 1638. When he married in 1643 he bore the title of 'painter and valet of the bedroom to the king'. He was one of the first members of the Académie royale de peinture et de sculpture founded in 1648. At Vaux he sported the title of first painter to the king which still belonged to Nicolas Poussin (1594-1665), and Poussin requested Foucquet's support in ensuring that he retained the title. Le Brun was officially granted the title only by Colbert, and not until 1664.

Foucquet might have preferred Poussin to Le Brun. But as we know after starting the galerie d'Hercule at the Louvre, the most celebrated French painter of the day had gone back to Italy with the firm intention of staying. When asked for advice in 1655 through the offices of Abbé Louis Foucquet who was then in Rome, Poussin stated 'that there was no one in painting who was tolerable and that he did

Portrait of Charles Le Brun (1619-1690) after Nicolas de Largillière

Before Foucquet took him on to decorate his château, Le Brun had been famous
for a few pictures and decorative schemes in Paris, e.g. at the Hôtel Lambert.
But his work at Vaux elevated his reputation to new heights,
probably earning him the title of first painter to the king,
a distinction confirmed by Colbert after Foucquet's arrest.

not even see anyone coming up and that the art was going to go into sudden decline'.[3] Even if Simon Vouet (1590-1649) had still been alive, Poussin would not have recommended an artist who had just filled Parisian town houses with sumptuous decorative schemes in a style so different from his own. As for Le Sueur, he had died that same year. Two rivals of Le Brun might have recommended themselves: Charles Errard (1606-89) who had been director of the Académie since 1647 and had already worked for the king, or Pierre Mignard (1621-95), a pupil of Vouet, who had just returned to France in 1657 after spending twenty years in Italy. Abbé Foucquet who regarded Mignard as 'the second painter of Rome' (after Poussin, of course) recommended him to his brother. If Mignard had come back with the Abbé in 1655 as he had planned to do, he would probably have been given the role at Vaux that fell to Le Brun. As we have seen, he may have painted a portrait of the Superintendent.[4] Giovanni Francesco Romanelli also had much to recommend him. He had been a pupil of Domenichino (1581-1641) and Pietro da Cortona (1596-1669), and had participated in decorating the Palazzo Barberini as well as producing important interiors for Mazarin and Anne of Austria ; but he left Paris in 1657 and returned to Italy to die. So in the end it was Le Brun who won the day. Moreover in the early 1650s he had been responsible for two decorative schemes which had attracted attention, at the Hôtel de La Rivière (now at the Carnavalet) and the Hôtel Lambert, where he had collaborated with Le Vau.

At Vaux Le Brun played the role of a prime contractor, supplying drawings for both the painted and the sculpted decoration. Such a role seems to have been unprecedented in the history of French art and anticipated the part he would play at Versailles. This supreme role is attested by many drawings which have been preserved. But it is possible that its extent may have been slightly overestimated. André Félibien and Madeleine de Scudéry who describe Le Brun's works credit him alone, while Le Brun himself, in charge of checking the money owed to the artists on the liquidation in 1661, recognized only artists working for him. A list of creditors which has fortunately been preserved cannot be regarded as an exhaustive list of the artists who worked at Vaux. In the eighteenth century it was believed that Le Sueur had played a part, and this cannot be completely ruled out ; and in the nineteenth century the dining-room ceiling was attributed to Mignard.[5] We will plead the cause of a few forgotten names. In any case a proper study of what is undoubtedly a masterpiece of French painting and sculpture has as yet only been partly done.[6]

Diagram identifying the subjects depicted in the salon

depicted in his palace ... the whole lower part of the picture is encircled by a large serpent representing the year ; on the serpent the months, weeks and days move round.' The four seasons were in position, with summer on the side of the gardens.[26] 'The hours, daughters of the sun, go up and down' the palace steps. The palace was surrounded by the gods of Olympus. Apollo or the sun was simply a representation of Cléomine, i.e Foucquet. His emblem, the squirrel, was a new star which formed the central culmination.[27] The palace of the sun as described by Ovid had already been depicted by Le Sueur in the *chambre des Muses* at the Hôtel Lambert, which Le Brun could use as a reference. But in its dimensions and profusion of detail the composition at Vaux, had it been carried out, would have been unprecedented in French art, and would undoubtedly have outshone the cupola at Val-de-Grâce, painted in 1663, which raised the reputation of Le Brun's rival Pierre Mignard to new heights.

The level of the salon that corresponds with the first floor of the château is decorated with sixteen sheathed figures bearing an emblem in the form of a medallion, on which the figures of the zodiac and the seasons can be identified.[28] The interpretation of the trophies used as overwindows is incomplete ; but emblems representing the continents[29] and some gods from Olympus[30] can be recognised. Madeleine de Scudéry who probably did not see the sculpted decoration did not relay Méléandre's commentary, which would have been very useful here in identifying eight or so of the figures. The sculptors whose names are not known worked after Le Brun's drawings.[31]

On the floor we can see the remains of a gnomon: sunlight streaming in through the central window to the south, would have struck the sundial. All in all, the salon was merely an amphitheatre between the court and the garden, completely open, where the great spectacle of nature unfolded.[32]

All the ground-floor rooms on the garden side have coved ceilings. The most famous, and justly so, is the *chambre des Muses*, the main room in the Superintendent's apartment. The coving and the ceiling it surrounds are a masterpiece of French painting. Le Brun put the knowledge he had gained in Italy to the test. André Félibien who described it at length writes: 'This room has a high vaulted ceiling in the fine manner described as Italian-style because it was in fact from Rome that we took the model for elevating our ceilings in this way.'

Central motif for the ceiling of the chambre des Muses

Initial scheme for the central motif on the ceiling of the chambre des Muses

Drawing by Charles Le Brun.

Chambre des Muses

(On left)

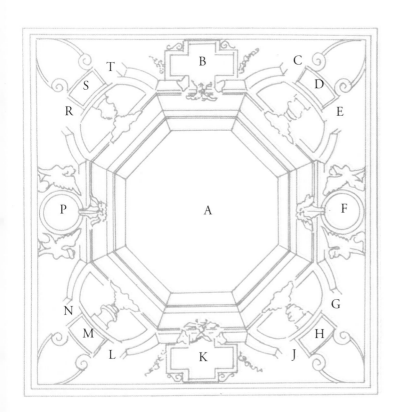

Diagram identifying the subjects depicted on the ceiling and coving in the chambre des Muses

A The triumph of Fidelity
B or K Nobility, Peace (unidentifiable)
C, E, G, J, L, N, R, T The Muses
(the ninth Muse Clio is in the central picture)
C Melpomene (tragedy)
E Thalia (comedy)
G Erato (love poetry)
J Polymnia (sacred song)
L Urania (astronomy)
N Calliope (epic poetry)
R Uterpe (music)
T Terpsichore (dance)
D, H, M, S The four categories of poetry
D Satiric poetry
H Lyric poetry
M Heroic poetry
S Rustic poetry
F Victory of the Muses over their rivals the Pierides
who are transformed into crows
P Victory of the Muses over the Satyrs

Thalia (comedy)

Coving in the *chambre des Muses*.

Alcove

Model by Jean Le Pautre. The alcove
in the *chambre des Muses*
which was never finished
should have been similar to this in appearance.

Polymnia

Drawing by Charles Le Brun
for the *chambre des Muses.*

Polymnia (sacred song)

Coving in the *chambre des Muses.*

The Muses' victory over the Pierides

Coving in the *chambre des Muses.*

Night

Ceiling of the alcove in the *chambre des Muses.*

The sciences and the arts

Overdoor in the *chambre des Muses.*

during the decade when Vaux was built that the latter was superseded by the former in grand houses. The French-style fireplace with its canopy extends quite a long way from the line of the wall ; the Roman-style or Italian-style fireplace which is contained in the thickness of the wall leaves only a fairly flat mantel visible. Fireplaces of this kind can be seen in all the rooms in the two apartments, often with the *garniture de cheminée* made for them in Foucquet's day.[37]

Thus the *chambre des Muses* like the salon is in the Italian style, or to be more precise the Roman style. Moreover, saying Roman rather than Italian perfectly reflects the experience of French artists in Italy, mainly acquired in Rome.

The *cabinet des jeux*, part of the Superintendent's apartment, is a room occupying half the area of a pavilion, with the other half containing a staircase ; but its decoration makes it a room of major importance. The ceiling is decorated with a figure of Sleep, a celebrated work painted by Le Brun. But the rest of the decorative programme, teeming with detail, full of putti and various animals, is no doubt by another artist, working under Le Brun's directions. We know that the small room was gilded by Gougeon known as La Baronnière who worked with Le Brun.[38] This decoration covers the coving and the panelling. Here it is not dado-height panelling, as in the *chambre des Muses*, but full-height panelling with pilasters, which was the usual practice in houses of the period where full-height wainscotting was used in small rooms. Unfortunately the panelling is not complete : a mirror recently replaced a portrait of the wife of Field Marshal de Villars which itself was an addition.

From the time of Foucquet's downfall, perhaps even before, it was noted that 'the squirrel was painted everywhere pursued by a grass snake which was the arms of Colbert', as Voltaire put it in *Le Siècle de Louis XIV* (1751). According to *Voyage pittoresque des environs de Paris* (1755) by Dezallier d'Argenville in this room you saw 'a squirrel which has beside it three lizards, the arms of Le Tellier, and a snake, the arms of Colbert, with the words 'Quo me vertam nescio' [I do not know who to turn to].'[39] The motif was supposedly invented by the painter 'twelve years after Foucquet's disgrace'. We know that all the Le Tellier and Colbert families had in common was that they had been in Mazarin's service and done Foucquet a disservice. In 1673, (exactly twelve years after his downfall), the creditors relinquished the Vaux-le-Vicomte domain to Madame Foucquet. Are

Ceiling and coving in the cabinet des jeux

In the centre, *Sleep* by Charles Le Brun.

Detail of the coving

Colbert's grass snake threatening Foucquet's squirrel.

The cabinet des jeux

Detail of a panel

Many of the figures and scenes which decorate this room have yet to be interpreted.

we to believe that a painter belatedly completed or altered this work? It seems doubtful that the comte de Vaux, Nicolas Foucquet's son, living in the château, would have financed a joke of this kind while the Superintendent was still in prison, but we cannot help being struck by the detailed nature of the information provided by Dezallier. There is another objection which appears more decisive – there is no trace today of the Latin motto. But this heraldic parable could have been located where the mirrors and pictures that have succeeded one another in the *cabinet des jeux* now hang, perhaps for the very purpose of replacing an image which could be interpreted all too easily by contemporaries. It is possible that Field Marshal de Villars who bought the château in 1705 was the censor: he owed his career to Louvois, a Le Tellier.[40] However that may be, the bestiary in the decorative programme dating from Foucquet's day, which does include the squirrel, snake, and lizard but also the toad, butterfly, peacock etc, cannot be reduced to mere ornament. Without finding precise references, we are reminded of the animals in La Fontaine's fables. There is no doubt that this menagerie is more than a simple feast for the eyes. For example there is a quite obvious play on the ambiguity of the snake, a symbol with many interpretations and part of Colbert's coat of arms. These snakes which recur in the decorative scheme of the gardens are explicitly identified in Pellisson's poem describing Le Nôtre's work as 'proud grass snakes ... which you want to approach but dare not'.[41] In the *cabinet des jeux* the two facing serpents on Mercury's caduceus are beside the lyre of Apollo. Mercury, we may remember, is the protector of both merchants and artists. The wand is depicted against olive or oak branches, symbols of peace and success which are again found on the façades of Vaux and in many contemporary portraits.[42] In the *cabinet de l'Amour* painted by Le Sueur at the Hôtel Lambert, we see pairs of snakes intertwined, facing one another, hanging by their tails, in every posture. There is no need to consult iconologies to recognize these as an evocation of amorous revels. On the façades of Vaux the two facing snakes are found with an arrow transfixing them. Yet on the coving of the *chambre des Muses* the two snakes, rather than facing one another, are turned towards the fleeing squirrel. The message was clear to the readers of *Clélie*, a *roman à clef*, where concerning the 'figures' at Vaux we read: 'What is remarkable is that there is not a single one that does not have a hidden meaning speaking of the virtues or glory of Cléomine, for those who know the meaning assigned to these various figures.'[43]

The ceiling of the *salon d'Hercule*, the antechamber of Foucquet's apartment, is decorated with a painting showing Hercules being welcomed by the gods of Olympus, and is the subject of a long commentary by Félibien who saw it as depicting the triumph of virtue, Foucquet's of course. The *en camaïeu* medallions and panels in the coving depict the labours of Hercules and a few other subjects the iconographical justification of which is not self-evident. As for the hangings, which in Foucquet's day narrated the story of Clytemnestra, they may have been only an interim solution, like those in the *chambre des Muses*. The paintings are definitely by Le Brun[44] who had already undertaken the task of treating the theme of Hercules at the Hôtel Lambert.

The king's room is mainly characterized by the presence of stucco winged figures at the corners of the coving, which explains why the room was initially called the *chambre des stucs*. The iconographic programme is not very coherent: Truth supported by Time on the ceiling, four virtues that might be described as royal in the lunettes, and a variety of subjects in the octagonal medallions. The surviving drawings prove that the total composition was by Le Brun.[45] According to Nivelon the stucco figures were made by Legendre and Girardon. The combination of stucco work and painting had been familiar in France since the creation of Francis I's gallery at Fontainebleau. The Jupiter room at the Pitti Palace in Florence, where there are stucco-work flying spirits 'very similar to those at Vaux' has been mentioned as a possible model.[46] Le Brun may have been more directly inspired by the apartments at the Louvre decorated by Anguier and Romanelli.

There is no mention of the king's room in *Clélie* which was apparently written before the scheme for it was executed, or even drawn up. The paintings on the ceiling and the coving were being carried out in July 1661.[47] The alcove remained unfinished, the painting for its ceiling was not installed, and no doubt the opening would have been decorated with columns and sculptures, like the one in the *chambre des Muses*. Foucquet had closed it off with a balustrade, as was right and proper for a royal alcove.[48]

Although visibly unfinished,[49] the antechamber and study completing the king's apartment are memorable for remarkable stuccoed covings, the work of an ornamenter, perhaps Cotelle.[50] There is almost no painting in these rooms.

Sequence of rooms in the state apartments

(Double page over)
The three rooms (the antechamber, main room and study) all lead into one another.
In the foreground the salon d'Hercule, the antechamber of Foucquet's apartment.

Ceiling of the salon d'Hercule

The *Apotheosis of Hercules*
by Charles Le Brun.
On the right, a victory
crowning Hercules.
Vice is crushed under the wheels
of the chariot, while Reason
is controlling the horses
which represent the passions.
Above Reason, Fame. In the sky
on the left, Jupiter, Juno and Diana
receive Hercules.

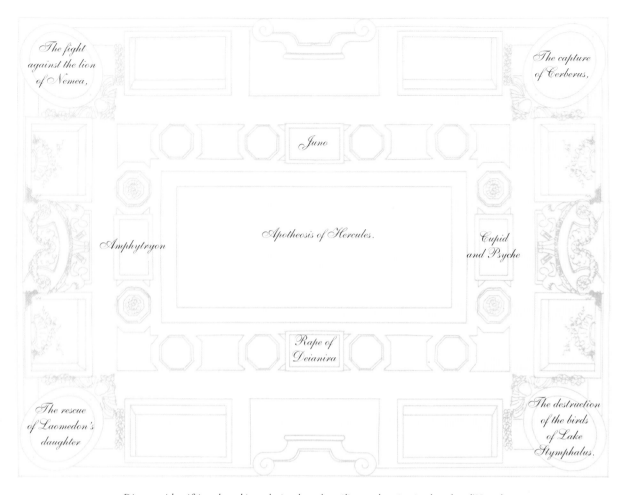

The fight against the lion of Nemea,

The capture of Cerberus,

Juno

Amphytryon

Apotheosis of Hercules.

Cupid and Psyche

Rape of Deianira

The rescue of Laomedon's daughter

The destruction of the birds of Lake Stymphalus.

Diagram identifying the subjects depicted on the ceiling and coving in the salon d'Hercule

Salon d'Hercule

In the foreground a table that formed part of Foucquet's furniture.

Female figure

Drawing by Charles Le Brun
for the Hôtel de la Rivière reused for Juno on a panel
on the coving in the *salon d'Hercule*.

Corner of the coving

Ceiling of the king's antechamber

The central motif, a fresco painting
(not cloth-backed like all Charles Le Brun's work),
was a later addition.

The king's antechamber (in the eighteenth century, library)

In the medallions on the coving:
Achilles asking Venus to return the shield
that Cupid has taken from him (above the fireplace).
Diana removing her shoes after hunting (opposite).
Cupid carrying Jupiter's thunderbolt (window side).
Cupid carrying a vine plant, pursued by a lion (opposite).

Alcove of the king's room

In the coving above the entrance into the alcove, Vertumnus.

Vertumnus

Coving above the entrance into the alcove in the king's room.

Stucco, winged figure

Coving of the king's room.

Winged figure

Drawing by Charles Le Brun.

Ceiling and coving in the king's room

Diagram identifying the subjects depicted in the ceiling and coving of the king's room

The description of the two large rooms overlooking the courtyard, neither of which has a coved ceiling, is tricky because of the ways in which they were refurbished or finished at a later stage.

Foucquet's dining-room has a coffered ceiling, built in a summary way, probably in a hurry so that it could take the eight pictures: in the centre *Peace restoring Plenty*, a composition by Le Brun which is usually seen as a reference to the Peace of the Pyrenees (1659), the culminating achievement of Mazarin's military and

Stucco motif from the ceiling of the king's study

Ceiling of the king's study

Unfinished decoration, possibly the work of Jean Cotelle.

Schemes for ceilings

Schemes by Jean Cotelle, 1640. Cotelle worked on the decoration of Vaux.

Central motif of the dining-room ceiling

Peace restoring Abundance by Charles Le Brun.

Decoration above the mirror in the dining-room

Trophy of War and (reflected) trophy of Peace.

diplomatic efforts ; around it are the four seasons and the four elements. Although these pictures are not of outstanding quality, they must nonetheless be at least partly Le Brun's work since a drawing by him for *Winter* has been preserved.[51] In his *Voyage pittoresque des environs de Paris* Dezallier d'Argenville noted: 'It is claimed that the tables were lowered from ceiling of this room magnificently served, and furthermore that a mist was previously released hiding them from the view of the guests.' Writing in 1785 Abbé Goudemetz added: 'On the ceiling screws can be seen by means of which the nectar of the gods and a thousand types of delicacies were lowered to tempt the monarch's appetite.' Bearing in mind the fact that the present installation of the ceiling is perfunctory, it cannot be ruled out that occasional tables were used for a time.

The full-height panelling which includes a few fine pieces with the emblems and monograms of Foucquet and his wife does not seem completely coherent. Rather mediocre *en camaïeu* paintings depicting the story of Io have been rather badly incorporated into it, perhaps at a later stage. It is hard to see what this episode from the loves of Jupiter – who transformed Io into a heifer so that she would escape Juno's wrath – is doing in the dining-room! The handsome trophies of War and Peace above the open arch leading to the serving room and the fireplace mirror, on the other hand, develop the theme of the central picture in the ceiling. The mirror has obviously been added. In its place Dezallier saw a painting of Louis XIII, and Nivelon a picture of Louis XIV placed in front of a portrait of Henry IV and trophies symbolizing in particular Rebellion chained by Amor, a reference to

One of the compartments in the dining-room ceiling

Winter.

Seated old man

Drawing by Charles Le Brun.

The dining-room

On the right, the sideboard. In the centre of the ceiling,
Peace restoring Abundance.
In the four rectangular ceiling compartments, Apollo or Fire, Diana or Air,
Flora or Ceres or Earth, Tritons and naiads or Water.
In the octagonal ceiling compartments, the four seasons.
In the circular or octagonal medallions on the wall, the story of Io.

Ceiling of Foucquet's bedroom on the first floor

This ceiling might be the work of Jean Cotelle.

the end of the Fronde and Louis XIV's marriage. Nivelon can be believed when he attributes that picture, now missing, to Le Brun, but not necessarily when he places it in this room, even though the subject is remarkably in line with that of the ceiling. The painting of Louis XIII must have replaced that of Louis XIV.

Again according to Nivelon, Le Brun painted a sideboard laden with food. Was it for the dining-room, or for the room next door? The serving room has a homogeneous decoration sometimes ascribed to Cotelle with landscapes attributed to Lallemand and unidentified scenes, which nonetheless seem to relate well to the theme of dining.

The large square room is the least finished of the ground-floor rooms. It is not even certain what it was intended for ; if we are to believe Félibien who stated that the *salon d'Hercule* was an antechamber for both the *chambre des Muses* and the large square room, it was apparently part of the Superintendent's apartment.

Diagram identifying the subjects depicted on the ceiling of Foucquet's bedroom

The walls are partly covered with wainscotting in which paintings depicting the battles of Field Marshal de Villars are set. The present arrangement dates from 1900.[52] In the lower part there are still remains of painting with the Foucquets' monogram. The high frieze is an *en camaïeu* painting which covers the window side of the room and has been extended by means of photographs over the other three sides. It depicts a Roman-style triumph and is usually attributed to Le Brun. It is tempting to associate it with a passage in Guillet de Saint-Georges ; he recounts how Le Brun after making a triumph of Constantine for Vaux which Mazarin admired when visiting the château was urged by the cardinal to emulate Raphael by painting a complete history of Emperor Constantine:[53] Le Brun did a battle and a triumph which 'have not been painted : but M. Audran has made engravings from the drawings'.[54] The drawings were also used as cartoons for the tapestries started at Maincy and completed at Gobelins. The engraved and woven triumph in no way resembles the frieze in the large square room. How long has it been there?[55] What was its purpose? It may be noted that it covers the area which would have been taken up by a coving if their room had been given one. The ceiling there today consists of a floor with beams and joists decoratively painted in the seventeenth-century style. As covings are no more than light shells suspended from a traditional floor, the room may have been waiting for coving to be installed, and the frieze could be just one of the decorations made in a hurry just before the official opening. Nonetheless the squirrel pursued by the grass snake was apparently seen on the joists in the eighteenth century, which would confirm that the French-style floor with exposed beams and joists was the final choice.[56] In Foucquet's day the walls were covered with six tapestries from a hanging depicting the story of Iphigeneia.

Upstairs only one room has retained its original decoration, the bedroom in Foucquet's private apartment. Wall hangings of the months which were part of the original decorative scheme have even been reinstated.[57] The ceiling of the alcove and that of the room have a *trompe-l'œil* decoration suggesting a cupola and a coving. The superb design of the frames and the painting of the panels can be attributed to Cotelle.

There are a few surviving fragments of the seventeenth-century decorative in the upstairs apartments which were much altered in the eighteenth century. Madame Foucquet's apartment was full of mirrors, in line with a fashion that emerged in the 1650s.[58] The panelling for the chapel located in the centre of the first floor, made by the joiner Jacques Prou after drawings by Le Brun and with Lespagnandel playing a role, was never installed, but it was put up in the chapel in the out-buildings and is still there.[59]

The interior decoration of Vaux owes its preservation, which all things considered is quite remarkable, to the fact that by its nature it is immovable or fixed ; even marks of the improvisation and unfinished state due to the events of 1661 have been preserved, and this is in spite of the obvious efforts made in the eighteenth and nineteenth century to camouflage them through pastiche and purchases. On the other hand it is much more difficult to form any idea of what the furniture was like. Only the two beautiful, large tables on display in the *salon d'Hercule* were part of the original furniture. Nonetheless a few conjectures and comments can be made. Much of the furniture used for the entertainments was brought in from Saint-

Ceiling of the alcove in Foucquet's bedroom

On either side of the false cupola, Dawn and Dusk.

Table that formed part of Foucquet's furniture

This table and its twin are the only furniture
that belonged to Foucquet still held at Vaux.

Mandé. This furniture removal was not an expedient ; up until the mid-eighteenth
century furniture was not assigned to one special house, it travelled with the person
who used it. The inventories highlight the very traditional nature of the 'furniture'
of Vaux, mainly textiles of every description – tapestries in particular. Now, as we
have seen, the subjects of the hangings installed did not coincide in any way with
the iconography, for all that it was so fastidious, and the overall decorative programme. Quite obviously in 1661 the furniture of Vaux was still on the loom.

The same observation applies to the external decoration: the works that were fix-
tures were preserved, while all those that could be moved without being damaged
were dispersed.
On the façade of the second level of the central projecting part of the building, on
the courtyard side, the design of the panelling for the chapel is reproduced on the
large pier against which the altar was placed, between the two round-headed windows. But the reclining figures on the pediment are entirely pagan: Apollo and

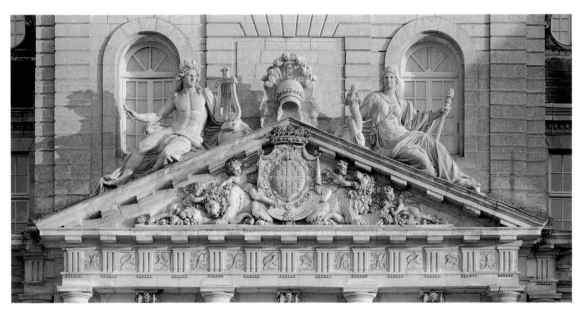

Pediment above the entrance of the courtyard side

The sculptures were made by Michel Anguier.

Rhea, the mother of Jupiter (or Cybele), the sky and the earth. The final composition, installed in the summer of 1659,[61] is the result of a scheme worked out from the drawings of Le Vau, Le Brun and Anguier who carried out the work.[61] There is no more telling example of the collaboration of the architect, painter and sculptor in the work carried out at Vaux.

According to Guillet de Saint-Georges, the Fame on the pediment of the façade on the garden side is by Poissant. The four standing statues that are the crowning feature of the first level of the projection on that façade are attributed to Anguier on the grounds that they are made of Vernon stone, a material which only Anguier would have used.[62] Fidelity can be recognized by her key and dog, Vigilance by her illuminated lamp and open book and Strength by her hand on her hip ; the fourth statue has not been identified.

On all the façades the metopes and window-tops are decorated with squirrels and Foucquet's monogram against oak or olive leaves. The medallions of Roman emperors on the spandrels of the projections are described as modern in the inventories. While they are certainly not antique, they seem nonetheless to have been reused. This probably also applies to the many busts that adorn both the main building and the pavilions in the outbuildings.

nandel, or rather it was, for most of it now dates from the nineteenth-century restoration. Lespagnandel's account of April 1659 mentions the 'icicles which are to surround the large figures of rivers', these figures themselves and the lions.[71] The herms must also be by him. The two reclining figures of the rivers Tiber and Anqueil are freely inspired by two famous antique sculptures of the Tiber and the Nile, often used as pendants both because of their history and through imitation.[72] The Tiber fared better in France than the Nile: the Roman river was reproduced in bronze and in marble for Francis I and Louis XIV, and was the only one kept at Vaux where it was boldly paralleled with the modest local river. This reflects the ambition often stated by the French and by Foucquet in particular to equal Roman models.

In front of the grotto there were 'on large pedestals the various parts of the world, depicted holding in their hands the most precious things from the countries they represent which they are bringing as a tribute to indicate that the whole earth has contributed towards embellishing this place'. We do not know who the sculptor of these four statues was, and they have disappeared (those now in situ are nineteenth-century additions).

A print by Silvestre shows a Hercules at the end of the view of the garden, as we have already said, identified through his pose with the Farnese Hercules, the famous antique sculpture preserved in Rome,[73] which inspired the making of the present statue added in the nineteenth century. In Foucquet's time the joiner Jacques Prou had made 'the model of the pedestal for the large Hercules with the steps surrounding it' following Le Brun's orders.[74]

The descriptions of Vaux finish with the Hercules. 'However, you must not imagine that I have described all the beauties of that place to you, for I assure you I have forgotten many of them,' Madeleine de Scudéry concludes. Her description could be no more than an interim account of a work 'still in its infancy': 'There is as much difference between what it is today and what it will one day be as between a pretty twelve-year-old-girl and how she will be when she is eighteen.'[75]

Fate and fortune

Vaux at the time of the Villars family • Vaux at the time of the Praslin family
Vaux at the time of the Sommier and Vogüé families
Vaux Roman-style
Vaux as a model for artists • Le Nôtre, a paragon of the French spirit

Châteaux rarely escape the fate consigning them to abandonment, dilapidation or revolution. The fact that Vaux has survived all three trials will amaze those who realise the full scale of the devastation wrought by them: large-scale destruction of the royal châteaux in Paris; the dispersal of the great decorative schemes of the Ile-de-France. Gone are the marvels of Rueil which Foucquet must have admired as he did all Richelieu's achievements; the château of Raincy, a prototype for Vaux, has been razed to the ground; the exceptional château de Meudon which had been further embellished by Servien, Foucquet's partner in the role of Superintendent, has been amputated. None of the magnificent interiors painted by Vouet is still in place. This is so much the case that the two momentous periods in the history of Vaux after Foucquet's downfall, namely the defence of the château during the Revolution by the duchesse de Praslin and its restoration by Alfred Sommier in the late nineteenth century, should belong in a general history of the French national heritage.

In 1673, ten years after the trial, the creditors finally relinquished Vaux to Madame Foucquet. Her eldest son Louis-Nicolas who bore the title of comte de Vaux came to live in the château. In 1684 he received it from his mother as a gift between living persons. He died in 1705. That same year his mother Madame Foucquet who outlived him sold the château to Field Marshal de Villars. In 1704 the architect François Bruant had drawn up 'very detailed plans ... of all the floors

Portrait of the wife of Field Marshal de Villars by Charles Coypel

Jeanne Angélique Roques de Varengeville
married Field Marshal de Villars in 1701.

Portrait of Field Marshal de Villars after Hyacinthe Rigaud

In 1705 Villars bought the château of Vaux-le-Vicomte
from Nicolas Foucquet's widow and it became Vaux-le-Villars.

of Vaux-le-Vicomte', apparently with no other motive than to prepare the sale;[1] fifteen years later he built the Paris town house of the comte de Belle-Isle, Foucquet's grandson, who later became a Field Marshal and a duke.[2]

In September 1705 Vaux became the Duchy of Villars, and in 1709 it was further elevated to a 'duché-pairie', making Villars a duke and a peer of the realm. As may be remembered, the famous Field Marshal owed his title of duke less to his victories in the War of the Spanish Succession than the way he subdued the Camisards in the Cévennes, and his title of peer of the realm to the bloody Battle of Malplaquet where he was gloriously defeated. The Battle of Denain (1712) through which Villars was to save the kingdom from invasion had not yet taken its place

Large square room

It is decorated with pictures
of Villars's battles mounted
in the wainscotting in 1900.
The frieze is a photographic
duplicate of the Le Brun drawing
which runs along the top of the wall
on the window side.

in the annals of history. On 14 August 1728 Villars received Queen Maria Leczinska, and on 20 July 1731 the king himself. The former apartment of the Superintendent which was made available to Louis XV then took on the name of the king's apartment. This transfer of the name from the left-hand apartment to the right-hand one resulted in a number of misunderstandings in the use of descriptions in the eighteenth century.

The battle pictures were of course Villars's main contribution to the decoration of Vaux. He had commissioned ten paintings from Jean-Baptiste Martin the elder. Only one of these pictures, *Le Siège de Fribourg*, has been preserved. What became of the other nine is not known. The five paintings now decorating the large square

Queen Maria Leczinska visiting Vaux in 1728

The tradition of royal visits which had started in the seventeenth century
carried on into the eighteenth century.

room, which was the billiard room in the Field Marshal's day, are by an unknown painter.[3] Villars had also asked a great artist to paint the most beautiful of his conquests, Jeanne Angélique Roques de Varengeville, whom he married in 1701 when she was nineteen and he was fifty. The portrait of Jeanne Angélique[4] by Charles Coypel (1694-1752) shows the object of the Field Marshal's affections, the magnet that attracted Voltaire who declared his love, and kept a small court in attendance at Vaux.

As a pointer to the way the art of garden design was to develop, lawns invaded the courts and replaced the *parterres de broderie* in the days of the Villars family. It is no accident that the guides at the same time indicate that the waterfalls and the 'grille d'eau' were in ruins. Worse still, duc Honoré Armand who inherited Vaux in 1763 on the death of his mother, (who had been a widow since 1734) apparently dug up the conduits for the fountains and sold the lead to pay his debts. If he was not the perpetrator of these depredations, they must be blamed on his successor, the duc de Praslin, who bought the château from him in 1764.[5]

Letters patent then transformed the Duchy of Villars into the Duchy of Praslin, for the benefit of the purchaser, César Gabriel de Choiseul, a cousin of the famous minister and himself given responsibility for Foreign Affairs in 1761 and the Navy in 1766. By a strange chance he commissioned the architect Jean-Baptiste Berthier with the Ministry for Foreign Affairs building, while as Secretary of State for War Field Marshal de Belle-Isle, Foucquet's grandson, had commissioned the same architect with the Ministry for War building. These two remarkable buildings stand side by side at Versailles near the château.[6] Berthier is better known as the author of the hunting map and the father of Field Marshal Berthier. In 1767 Berthier senior replanned the first floor at Vaux, almost completely demolishing Foucquet's private apartments.

Praslin did not alter the state apartments; he only furnished the antechamber of the stuccoed apartment with book cases – beautiful as they are, they must nonetheless have destroyed part of the original decorative programme. No doubt a new decorative scheme for the large square room – which did not prove to be lasting – can be attributed him, clearing out the battle scenes which were reinstated in 1900. In a description dated 1785 we find this strange note regarding that room: 'The ceiling and everything decorating the billiard room is based on the century and taste of Francis I. It is a repetition of Francis I's gallery at Fontainebleau.'[7] The important collection of Louis XVI furniture disposed of by the Praslins at the Hôtel Drouot auction rooms in 1876, just after the sale of the château, must have been furniture commissioned for Vaux by duc César Gabriel.

He also created a picturesque garden to the north of the entrance to the château, taking advantage of the winding course of the stream before it enters the gardens *à la française*. This is usually attributed to César Gabriel's grandson, but wrongly since the presence of the 'pretty English-style walks on this side of the château' is attested in the 1785 description.[8] Whether the sale of the conduits was the work of Villars or Praslin does not alter the fact that the eighteenth century was distinguished by a slow turning away from gardens *à la française*, although Le Nôtre's reputation remained high throughout the century.

We think the creator of the 'Francis I' decorative scheme and the new garden can be identified as one of the most famous artists of the day – the architect Charles de Wailly (1730-98). He actually drew up a general plan of the château of Vaux in 1784, no doubt in preparation for a major scheme.[9] The fine perspective views drawn by him must also date from this time.

Portrait of César-Gabriel de Choiseul-Praslin by Alexandre Roslin's studio

Praslin bought Vaux from Field Marshal de Villars's son in 1764.

Vaux-le-Vicomte

Drawing by Charles De Wailly. It would seem this architect working for the duc de Praslin made
changes at Vaux of which there is no longer any trace.

Duc Renaud-César-Louis, the son and heir of César Gabriel, died in 1791. It was his wife who defended the threatened château along with the interests of their son Antoine-César, imprisoned in 1793. Having been warned of its imminent destruction based on a requisition issued by the procurator syndic of Melun, she addressed a memorandum to the temporary Commission for the Arts, set up by the Convention to safeguard monuments and works of art from the châteaux and churches: 'It is to be believed that the Procurator Syndic's requisition has been dictated by the law ordering the demolition of fortresses and castles with towers, bastions, battlements that might lead to the fear that they could become places of refuge for enemies of the Republic. None of these provisions applies to the château de Praslin. Lying on low ground, the building is overlooked on all sides; it does not have a single tower, not so much as a turret; the walls are pierced on all sides with a large number of windows, and never did the architect who built it think of fortifying it.' If the decision to destroy the building was not withdrawn, however, the duchesse asked for a stay of execution to take down the paintings by Le Brun and Le Sueur *(sic)* which she intended to give to the Museum.[10] On 25 Frimaire Year II (of the French Revolutionary calendar), the commissioners sent to Vaux by the Commission submitted a report arguing in favour of preserving it. The château escaped with just the destruction of a few coats of arms and symbols in the first flush of enthusiasm of the Revolution.

Under the next duke who survived the Revolution and died in 1808 and his son Charles-Raynaud-Laure-Félix who died in 1847, it would appear that no attempts were made to arrest the deterioration of the château. 'The duc de Praslin lived there so parsimoniously that nothing could be sadder or more dilapidated,' according to an account written *c.*1820. 'The water towers were no longer in existence; potatoes were growing in Le Nôtre's parterres; the statues and marble vases were lying overturned and mutilated. In the magnificent salle des gardes [the salon] where Fouquet had received Louis XIV piles of sacks of grain, disused furniture, old sedan chairs and even a small carriage could be seen. In one corner was the hum of a class of little girls. The duchesse de Praslin was teaching them to read and hearing their catechism.'[11] The duc had in fact founded an elementary school in the outbuildings of the château. It is true that in 1835 he had also asked Charles Séchan to design a composition for the cupola in the salon, but the result is very pedestrian. Yet it seems he had turned to the architect Louis Visconti (1791-1853) who apparently decorated the bathroom in 1834-1836[12] and remade decorations in the seventeenth-century manner here and there, no doubt to fill in gaps. It is more probable that this commission can be attributed to his son duc Théobald who declared

Cupola of the bathroom

It was decorated between 1830 and 1840 by the architect Louis Visconti.

his intention of restoring the château. In 1842 Visconti remade the lantern of the dome.[13] Was he assisted or had he been replaced by the architect François Hippolyte Destailleurs who restored the grotto in 1845?[14] The duc de Praslin who supported the Orleanist branch of the royal family received King Louis-Philippe at Vaux – who had himself started work on restoring Versailles. The murder of the duchesse and the duc's suicide in 1857 brought work at Vaux to an end.

The place was completely abandoned until it was bought by the industrialist Alfred Sommier in 1875. 'At that date M. Guyot de Villeneuve, the renowned bibliophile whose collection of books was famous, was Prefect of Seine-et-Marne,' Alfred's son Edme Sommier wrote. 'He invited one of his friends M. Alfred Sommier, knowing him to be a great lover of art and history, to come to Melun as he wanted to show him this house of Vaux before it finally disappeared – for it was thought that was bound to be its fate; it was relatively forgotten at that time but had had its hour of fame, and was regarded as being condemned. During that visit M. Alfred Sommier had the impression that the condition of the château was far from being as bad as was generally thought; he was particularly struck to see all the decorations by Le Brun more or less intact. At that point he was looking for a property as his family home at Montmorency had been sacked during the siege of Paris. A few days later, bringing an architect with him to check his own first impressions, he returned to examine the place. It then seemed to him that it was completely possible to preserve the château, and from the artistic point of view it was an interesting undertaking. On 6 July 1875, the day appointed for the sale, he turned out to be the sole bidder.'

He entrusted the task of restoring Vaux to the architect Gabriel Hippolyte Destailleurs (1822-93), the son of the Destailleurs who had worked on the grotto in 1845. For the restoration of the garden Destailleurs was assisted by Elie Lainé.[15] Destailleurs was known as a scholar, a collector of architectural drawings and the restorer of many châteaux and mansions throughout Europe.[16] Since 1873 he had been in charge of restoring the château of Courances, near Vaux. Among his most outstanding historicist creations the château de Franconville (1876), imitating Maisons, and Waddeston Manor (1874-89) built for the Rothschilds should be mentioned. At Waddeston Manor in England, his collaborator for the gardens was the same Elie Lainé who is not known for any other project.[17] When Destailleurs died in 1893 the bulk of the restoration work had been completed.[18]

Alfred Sommier

After buying Vaux
from the heirs of the Praslin family in 1875
he commissioned Gabriel Hippolyte
Destailleurs and Elie Lainé with the general
refurbishment of the place.

Important, tricky strengthening work (remaking the wall between the king's antechamber and main room from top to bottom; replacing wooden floors with metal-framed floors above the coved ceilings) had been carried out in the château which had also been refurnished. The outbuildings on the right had been closed off with a wing on the site that Foucquet's audience chamber should have occupied. The garden buildings had been restored, or even rebuilt (in the case of the waterfalls), and the gardens themselves were refurnished with statues.[19]

In spite of the huge expense (five and a half million gold francs), the work could not really be regarded as finished on Alfred Sommier's death in 1908. Could it ever be? Because of the difficulty of the undertaking Alfred Sommier had decided against reinstating the waterway. His son Edme Sommier called on Achille Duchêne, a great restorer and imitator of gardens *à la française*, to complete the reinstatement of the gardens. Duchêne created the beds at the sides of the main building (1910) and the *parterres de broderie* (1923).[20]

On his marriage to Christina Colonna in 1967 Patrice de Vogüé, the great-grandson of Alfred Sommier and Edme's great-nephew, was given the château by his father. The Vogüés are a very old family, and the château bearing their name is in Vivarais. In former times a Charlotte de Vogüé had been a keen visitor to the little court at Vaux formed round her sister-in-law, the wife of Field Marshal de Villars. The château was in good condition in 1967, but considerable sums of money were required for its upkeep. The obvious solution was to open it to the public.

The young owner took over as head one of the most sizeable of those businesses which were starting to develop at the gates of château. Will it last? The costs of running Vaux are balanced only if there are 300,000 visitors a year. That figure was reached for the first time in 1989, a lucky year; since then it has continued a little below that level. Patrice de Vogüé could legitimately congratulate himself on having saved Vaux for a second time, making do with paltry assistance from the state (5 francs for each visitor to Vaux as against approximately 2,000 francs for every person who attends the Opera!).

But there are new threats on the horizon. The surrounding area is changing. On average 2,000 hectares of agricultural land in the department are transformed every year into building plots. In these circumstances the protection of the area within 500 metres of historic monuments may well be ineffective. Also there is increasing insecurity; criminal acts, which are not followed up and therefore remain unpunished, make it necessary to resort to private security organizations.

State of the gardens c.1875

The gardens were uncultivated when Alfred Sommier bought Vaux.

Seventeenth-century sculptures

Cupid carrying a basket:
a group originating
from the château of Maisons,
attributed to Philippe de Buyster.
These statues dating
from the same period as Foucquet
which Alfred Sommier
bought for Vaux illustrate the genre
for roguish children, or 'marmousets',
which Le Nôtre had introduced
at Vaux and developed at Versailles.

Nineteenth-century sculptures

The gardens were refilled with statues commissioned from contemporary sculptors by Alfred Sommier.
Opposite: *Rape of Europa* sculpted by Hiolle, 1886.
Below: *Seahorses and children* sculpted by Alfred Lanson, 1880.

Beds at the side of the château

These were designed by Achille Duchéne in 1910.

To dissipate the shadows of the present, let us listen to the judgement of the muse of History up there on the ceiling of the *chambre des Muses*. If we go by the terms used when Vaux was created, it is apparently a completely Roman creation: the salon, the covings, the alcoves and the fireplaces are all Roman-style; *Clélie* is sub-titled a 'Roman story'; the orange and lemon trees came from Rome; and the Tiber is featured beside the canal. The subjection of French art to the Roman model has never been more loudly proclaimed, if not more real, than during Mazarin's term as a Minister. 'If you wanted to send the plans for your houses and your gardens to have them checked over a little by the skilful people here, it might be useful to do so,' Abbé Foucquet wrote to his brother from Rome regarding the schemes for Vaux.[21] We know that Le Vau's schemes for the Louvre were sent to Rome to obtain the opinion of the Roman masters, Gianlorenzo Bernini (1598-1680) in particular. When he came to France, the judgement he gave on Le Brun's scheme for the

Parterres de broderie in front of the château

They were turfed over in the eighteenth century and reinstated only in 1923 by Achille Duchêne.

cupola of the salon was deferentially noted down: '*E bello, ha abbondanza senza confusione*' (It is beautiful, it has abundance without confusion).[22]

Yet the river Anqueil is the pendant of the Tiber in the grotto. Contemporaries hailed Foucquet's achievement as the first demonstration of the superiority of French art. La Fontaine saw Le Brun as the 'rival of artists like Raphael', the 'successor of men like Appelles through whom our climate owes nothing to the Roman one'; of Molière whose developing fame he admired he says: 'From the way in which his name spreads / It must be beyond Rome'.[23] The anonymous witness of the entertainment of 17 August 1661 writes: 'Tivoli and Frascati and everything beautiful, magnificent and amazing which Italy boasts of possessing must admit that it has nothing to compare with Vaux.'[24]

We must believe that Europe was convinced. Sir Christopher Wren (1632-1723) when he came to France in 1665, as much to meet Bernini as to study French architecture, admired 'The incomparable villas of Vaux and Maisons'.[25] Sir John Vanbrugh (1664-1726) must have seen Vaux when he travelled to France. Blenheim Palace and Castle Howard, two major works of English architecture, borrow several things from the French château: the combined terrace and flight of stairs, the incurvation of the low wings, the double staircase ascending on either side of the hall. The British lion strangling the gallic cock in its paws at the entrance of Blenheim (built for Marlborough, Villars's adversary at Malplaquet) seems to us to be a parody of the lion at Vaux, which really was preparing to smother the squirrel it was embracing.

Several generations of Swedish architects and art lovers have taken an interest in French architecture to such an extent that they have assembled in Stockholm a collection of drawings that is one of the main sources for studying the architecture of Louis XIV's reign. As no inventory is yet available, finding things in this collection is a matter of chance, and proof that Nicodemus Tessin (1654-1728) and Carl Harleman visited Vaux, though apparently interested only in the grotto, is among such chance discoveries. However Tessin, the architect of Charles XII of Sweden, did admit that he had borrowed from Vaux the oval salon of the château he built at Roissy in France (1697).[26]

During the same period the German architect Christoph Pitzler visited the gardens of Vaux.[27] Throughout the eighteenth century the large salon forming a projection in front of the building, the only more or less identifiable mark of Le Vau's influence, would be found in Germany. It can be seen at the Residenz in Würzburg, which Johann Neumann (1687-1753) built after consulting French masters and at Schloss Solitude, the work of Pierre-Louis-Philippe de La Guêpière (1715-73), as well as elsewhere.

Regarding the paintings at Vaux the duchesse de Praslin who, as we have seen, attributed them to both Le Sueur and Le Brun wrote: 'Strangers often come here to consult the drawings of these great masters and the finished pieces which are always admired for the vigour of their touch, the freshness of their colour and the sublimity of their brushwork.'[28]

We know how much the reign of Louis XIV was admired in the eighteenth century, particularly by Voltaire. The example of the masters who worked on Versailles was invoked in France against the style known as Rococo, or the decadence of the arts, arguing in favour of a return to the grand taste. 'Since this famous artist's death,' we read in the *Encyclopédie* regarding Le Nôtre, 'the art he invented has degenerated strangely among us, and of all the tasteful arts it is perhaps the one which has lost most in our days. Far from building on his great and beautiful ideas, we have totally abandoned the good taste of which he had given us the example and the principles'.[29] Turfing over the surfaces at Vaux is one of the demonstrations of this evolution in taste, which between 1760 and 1770 gave rise to the picturesque garden imitated from English models, even at Vaux.

Le Vau's reputation in France did not keep pace with Le Nôtre's. The oval salon projecting from the main building on the garden façade admittedly became a convention; but it became commonplace so quickly and totally that Le Vau's name did not remain associated with it. Moreover, except for the salon, everything that went into making the architecture of Vaux fell into disuse: the brick and stone course work, the pavilions, the combined terraces and flights of stairs, the high roofs and the painted covings. It would be nice to know the comments made by the Académie d'architecture on the plans of Vaux presented by Bruant in 1704; that they 'gave rise to discussion on the construction and the general layout of large country houses,' is all that the minutes tell us.[30] But Jacques-François Blondel (1705-74), the theorist of French-style architecture whose teaching carried great weight in the decades between 1740 and 1770 and the early 1770s, did express his views on the château of Vaux. Most of his criticisms apply only to the scheme shown in Marot's engraving which, as we have said, inadvertently or otherwise he takes for the scheme carried out.[31] But some criticisms hit the mark and the main conclusion is that Blondel did not think Vaux was worth visiting.

It is the line of descent from the two Mansarts that seems to have been the basis for the seventeenth-century art that was taken over by the eighteenth century. Although Maisons is in many ways less modern than Vaux, it was there that Blondel took his pupils every year to teach them to admire the manner of François Mansart, the 'god of architecture'.[32] All in all prejudice did not favour Le Vau. Yet he played too important a role in the first half of Louis XIV's reign for his reputation to fail to attract followers. Thus Blondel thought it necessary to warn against this imitation. He concludes his criticism of Vaux with a caution: 'All the lapses deserve to be noticed all the more as Le Vau's reputation alone can mislead the credulity of young architects who, not yet being in a position to dispute the opinions of the master of the Art, copy them down to their errors, and based on such examples barely succeed in producing corrupt, foolhardy compositions.'

Scheme by Charles De Wailly for the Palazzo Spinola in Genoa, 1773

The work of Charles De Wailly who was at Vaux in 1784 is a good demonstration of Vaux's influence.

Nonetheless the young architects emerging from the school in the 1770s displayed a desire for emancipation which opened up all the paths between the extremes represented by classicism inspired by Antiquity and the picturesque. Charles de Wailly, a pupil of Blondel, was the most prominent representative of this eclecticism. The views he drew when called in to work at Vaux in 1784 are quite obviously the work of an admirer. The château of Montmusard (1764-1769), one of the most typical buildings designed by the new school, proves that De Wailly was familiar with Vaux before working on it.

The scheme that won the *Grand Prix de l'Académie d'architecture* in 1776, the work of Jean-Louis Desprez, a brilliant architect and De Wailly's junior, is a cross between Vaux and Maisons. The competition programme could be a description of Vaux: competitors had to design 'a château for a great lord consisting of a large main building preceded by courts, forecourts and avenues; accompanied by two separate groups of buildings for the stables and coach houses and for the kitchens in the outbuildings. The main building will be double'... The roof space must be 'apparent and of a noble form and decoration suitable for this special type of building ... ' Finally, among other things, they had to envisage a 'dining-room which is not an antechamber'.[33]

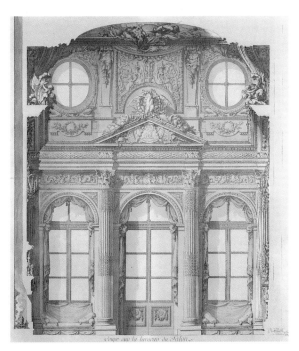

Scheme by Charles De Wailly for the salon at the Palazzo Spinola in Genoa, 1773

The Spinola salon is of course in the Italian style: but in it we find the coving with stucco figures,
the painted ceiling and several motifs from the decorative scheme at Vaux.

The commissioners from the Commission for the Arts who argued in favour of
preserving Vaux, after a few criticisms regarding the detail of the composition,
came to a conclusion which must have met with approval by contemporaries: 'We
observe [that this château] was built in 1668 [*sic*] at the start of the renaissance of
the arts in France and that it is one of the most beautiful houses for that period.'

The condemnation of Vaux in 1661 had thus to some extent been quashed. But
full and complete rehabilitation still took some time. The nineteenth century was
still critical of an architecture it regarded as too heavy.[34] The collections of prints
which proliferated to form an illustrated anthology of the monuments of France
could not ignore such an important residence, but the engravers gave an ungrace-
ful impression of it.[35] People's interests lay elsewhere, as illustrated by Vaux's
absence from *Voyages pittoresques* by Taylor and Nodier whose inspired lithographs
depict ruined castles in wild sites.

There were indications of a discreet return to the grand French manner during the
Second Empire. But that movement benefited mainly Ange-Jacques Gabriel

(1698-1782), who was moreover a perfect heir to the Mansarts. Thus Alfred Sommier's choice of Vaux in 1875 was still ahead of its time. In 1888 the architect Rodolphe Pfnor published his remarkable monograph on the château with an essay by Anatole France. The eclecticism prevalent in 1900 had its codes: the large châteaux that industrialists were building in the Ile-de-France and Sologne had to be in the French style, i.e. a style ranging from Louis XIII to Louis XVI. On the eve of World War I a return to traditions was carried along on the wave of nationalism. Le Nôtre was seen as the paragon of the French spirit.[36] Where this is concerned the crucial reference is Lucien Corpechot's book, *Les jardins de l'intelligence*, published in 1912 and reissued in 1937, two significant dates. 'During the years when Le Nôtre studied painting and architecture, the flower of French classicism, nurtured by all the sap of our soil, was preparing to burst open. The development of purely indigenous and original qualities would end up in the burgeoning of an art that is so general and so stripped of particularity, an art so suited to satisfying the spirit and its everlasting demands, that after three centuries, it has not ceased to delight mankind.'[37] To our eyes this theory suffers from the genetic taint relating to all theories which tend to make us believe that there is an order underlying the flourishing of the arts, and succeed in doing so at the cost of some simplifications or manipulations. Thus, as far as Corpechot is concerned, if Corneille had been a gardener he would have worked in the manner of Le Nôtre![38]

A masterpiece such as the château of Vaux-le-Vicomte is a polyhedron. To understand it we have to observe every side of it in succession. But what is there to be gained by describing its regularity as Classical, or its irregularities as Baroque? We are still awaiting a definition of Baroque that is applicable to French art. If Classicism is reduced to the theory of art regarded as a universal language, it can be said of that militant ideology which produces standards on paper that it has remained confined to treatises and has never prevented deviations (Mannerism, Baroque, Rococo etc) from proliferating. How simple everything would have been if the commissioners responsible for the 1661 inventories had labelled each item!

Beyond the canal

Two of the four parts of the world, sculpted by Peynot in the 1880s.

Index

Index of proper names used in the main text
(Names of people in Roman type, names of places in bold)

Colour reproduction by AD VER / JOB COLOR, Milano
Printed by Grafiche Alma, Milano

Paraphé; Ne varietur p.
L'arresté; suid ce Jourdhuy

Fouquet

Paraphé suiuant l'arrest